# CREATING MAGICKAL ENTITIES

## A COMPLETE GUIDE TO ENTITY CREATION

David Michael Cunningham
with
Taylor Ellwood & Amanda R. Wagener

Egregore Publishing
Perrysburg, OH

FIRST EDITION

Cataloging-in-Publication Data
Cunningham, David Michael.
Creating magickal entities: a complete guide to entity creation / David Michael Cunningham with Taylor Ellwood and Amanda R. Wagener. 1st—ed.
p. cm.
Includes bibliographical references and index.
ISBN 1-932517-44-8
1. Magic. 2. Spirits—Miscellanea. 3. Evocation—Miscellanea.
I. Ellwood, Taylor II. Wagener, Amanda R. III. Title
Library of Congress Control Number: 2003107760
133-dc21

Any trade names, trade marks, service marks, etc. mentioned in this publication are for identification only. Therefore, any specific company or product mentioned is owned by their respective owner and not by Egregore Publishing. Further, the company or product mentioned neither owns, endorses, nor has heard of Egregore Publishing. By stating this, we can avoid printing the ®, ™, ©, etc. marks that we might otherwise have to place throughout the text.

The publisher does not participate in, endorse, or have any authority or responsibility concerning private business transactions between our authors and the public.

Published by
    Egregore Publishing
    PO Box 572
    Perrysburg, OH 43552-0572

    info@EgregorePublishing.com
    www.EgregorePublishing.com
    (888) 771 - 5453

Printed in the United States of America

# DEDICATION

This book is dedicated to the teachers and mentors that have shared their magickal wisdom with us and many others. This book is also dedicated to those that are starting and continuing their studies and practices of the occult arts. If it were not for such people, we would not have anyone to share our knowledge with.

David personally dedicates this book to his mother, for teaching him that he is the master of his own reality.

Taylor personally dedicates this book to Matthew Thompson, Storm Constantine, Todd Heilmann, and to the Magick.

Amanda personally dedicates this book to the memory of "Robot," her mother, father, and her brother Aaron for accepting her uniqueness (and who keep the memory of Robot alive still to this day).

# ACKNOWLEDGMENTS

Thanks to our mentors, families, friends, and fellow magi for the contributions that they have made to this book. Without their lust for tried and tested knowledge and their belief that we could satisfy this lust, we wouldn't have been challenged to put our knowledge in a format so that others may learn from our experiences.

We wish to express our gratitude to Phil Hine, Donald Michael Kraig, and Patricia Telesco, for helping us in both magick and writing.

To Storm Constantine, Douglas Grant, Chris Chenette, Richard Sutherland II, and Bryan Lee Briggs, we owe a world of thanks.

David personally thanks Sensei Joseph Hurtsellers of the Academy of Karate by Hurtsellers, Toledo, Ohio (www.academyofkarate.com). Through his instruction and caring as a teacher, Mr. Hurtsellers has provided David with the tools to command focus and dedication in his life.

Taylor would like to thank David and Amanda for their support in this book.

Amanda thanks her husband for his support and understanding. She also thanks Mrs. Jennifer Kiernan and the late Mr. John Harlow, her high school English/Creative Writing instructors, for encouraging her to be creative, providing an environment to stretch her mind, and a kick in the rear when she needed it.

# DISCLAIMER

This book is designed to provide information in regard to the subject matter covered. It is sold with the understanding that the publisher, authors, contributors, and advisors are not rendering legal, medical, psychological, or other professional services or advice.

It is not the purpose of this book to reprint all the information that is otherwise available to readers but to compliment, amplify, and supplement other texts. For more information, please see the references at the end of this book.

Every effort has been made to make this book as complete and accurate as possible. However, there may be mistakes both in content and typography. The publisher accepts no legal or otherwise responsibility for the contents therein. The opinions of the author and contributors do not necessarily reflect those of the publisher.

The publisher, authors, contributors, and advisors shall have neither liability nor responsibility to any person or group of people with respect to any loss or damage caused or alleged to be caused directly or indirectly by the information contained in this book.

If you do not agree with and do not wish to be bound by the above, you may return this book to the publisher for a full refund.

# CONTENTS

# DEFINITION OF ENTITY

In this book you will learn how to create a magickal entity and how to use that entity to help you in life. One of the first things we must do, before we can begin, is to define what an entity is. For the purpose of this book, the term entity shall be defined as: *a vital principle held to give life to an immaterial essence, which has been created to have a self-contained and distinct existence with a conceptual reality, by the deliberate effort of personifying segregated thoughts and emotions.* In other words, you have the ability to create a "being," from the thoughts and emotions of your conscious mind, and by your direction this "being" will act to manifest your desires. An entity combines the essence of the desired result with that of the person that created the entity. Unlike some forms of magickal workings, such as the creation of a talisman, entities are aware of their environment and understand its sense of purpose.

The entities that can be created, through the help of this book, are thought-forms that have been selected to bring forth desired results. A thought-form is a symbol that represents a concept or thought for the person. A thought-form can be visualized by anyone and can represent anything. It is entirely in the realm of concept until the person makes the thought-form manifest into reality. That can be done through entity work as well as other methods. Through the deliberate actions and intentions of segregation and personification (separating the essential idea away from everyday concerns and giving it a personality, special characteristics, and associations to symbols), the thought-forms will take on a conceptual form that will allow them to maximize the energy that they have received through your actions and intentions. By maximizing this energy you allow for very powerful actions to occur through creative processes.

All things that are created with the mind have the ability to manifest outside of the mind in some form or shape. The mind is a microcosm of the universe. That which affects the mind, has the ability to affect the universe.

People have created and worked with different types of entities far beyond recorded history. Many gods and goddesses came into being as thought-forms personified. This allowed humans to interact with and interpret cause and effect in the world in which they lived. Often these fledgling thought-forms were slowly transformed into the gods and goddesses that we know today by the general acceptance of the attributes given to events. As more people adopted those understandings of the events as actions of "things greater than themselves," the thought-forms gained momentum and energy from the people that understood them. Over time a single thought had transformed from one person's way of understanding the world, to what are now considered some of the most powerful gods, goddesses, demons, and spirits.

When someone says the word "familiar," images of a witch's black cat often come to mind. A "familiar" entity often aids witches in magickal workings. Sometimes they will help lend a hand in regards to an upcoming event. What most people don't know is that the cat isn't the "familiar". The entity attached to the cat is the familiar. The "familiar" uses the cat as a medium so that it can effect the world around it and help the mage in his or her work. Even fewer people know that "familiars" are often created, and that witches are not the only people that create entities similar to "familiars." Since ancient times the belief and use of entities, such as "familiars," have been wide spread. Often people would house these entities in things other than cats, such as bottles, gems, statues, etc.

By taking specific thoughts and emotions and identifying them with things like names, symbolic attributes, etc., we are better able to work with them in a conscious manner. Therefore it is very important that we wisely choose our thoughts and the way that we understand them. If we do not understand our thoughts and emotions and try to use them for our own benefit, the results can, and more often than not, will be counterproductive.

Some people question the reality of entities created by our thoughts and emotions. Their understanding is that if we have the ability to create something with our mind, it therefore must be imaginary. This is, however, not the case. When someone studies magick long enough, they will come to the understanding that what is thought of as "self" and "not self" is merely an illusion. We only have company in life due to the illusion of being separated. Everything that we experience, perceive, or understand in any way, has been created within our own minds. The world as we understand it was created by us through our experiences. The world that we live in is only that of ourselves. Only we have the ability to change the things in our world, and our mind gives us the ability to do just that.

Everyday we, as evolving humans, learn something new. When we are presented with a new situation, we do our best to relate to this experience with the knowledge that we already have. As time goes on, we may find that our original thoughts and theories may have been incorrect and need to be changed a bit. We do not discard the experience all together as though it never happened. What we do is note what we have learned and adjust our understanding accordingly. Everything in the world as we know it has been constructed by the limitations of our own minds at the time that we experienced it. Thereafter, we merely build upon our own thought constructions for what we perceive to be "real" or the "truth." Once you understand how to change your perceptions, there is nothing in this world that your mind cannot change.

In relation to entities, this simply means that we really may not know exactly what entities are, but we know that they exist. As we learn more about them through our interaction and practice of working with them, we adapt what we have learned to fit into our new understandings or our experiences.

It is important to not discard the validity of any type of entity just because we do not understand it or have evidence supporting it. Rather, we must accept our experiences and understand that we are only limited by our experiences. The more we learn about a subject, in this case entities, the more that they come into our realm of understanding, much like the American Continents did for Europeans that were unaware of their existence.

You create entities and can accordingly determine what such entities will do for you. You don't use the perception of belief with entities, but instead use the perception of attributes with your entity. To put it simply, you choose to perceive that an entity has specific talents about it that will help in your operations. Those talents are attributes that you have placed upon the entity. A thing to understand about entities is that they have different levels of intelligence. This intelligence depends on the type of entity.

One way of understanding entities is that they are formed from the collective unconscious. When we specifically identify and give a certain type of energy human attributes, we are separating the energy from the collective unconscious and create a new being. This new being is still interconnected with the collective unconscious, as we all are, but it is a distinct energy being.

Entities have the ability to draw on the collective unconsciousness when they are instructed to do so. By doing this, entities are able to learn new skills and gain information. This ability also allows for them to affect the collective unconsciousness in ways that will allow for their tasks to be accomplished.

If entities are formed from thoughts and emotions, what were they before they were formed? There are many different theories and understandings on this topic. Most of the theories seem to make a reference to a great mass of energy. Some often refer to this mass as the Creative Life Force. This energy, or Life Force, exists in all things and expands beyond human understanding. When a human decides to give a part of this great energy mass a form, it establishes this small part of energy as a new spiritual being. This new spiritual being resides on a plane of existence that some magickal practitioners refer to as the astral plane.

The process is similar to when parents conceive a child. They take a part of the Great Creative Life Force and give it a form. This new form exists on both the astral and physical planes. An identity is established and furthers the creation of this being. The original energy from the Creative Life Force has not been separated from the rest, but it has been provided with an astral and physical "container" in which it can reside.

One way to look at it is to think of the thought, emotion, or both, as the equivalent to the male's semen. The Creative Life Force is thought to be the female's egg. When the two join, they form a being that combines the genetic code of both parts. This genetic code is the driving force and guide by which the entity shall "live its life."

This is similar to the process of entity creation. You create an astral "container" for the great Creative Life Force on the astral world. Even though a portion of the Creative Life Force has been separated, it is still interconnected with the greater whole of the Creative Life Force.

# ENTITY USES

The creation of magickal entities can be a very rewarding form of magickal working. One thing that people tend to state, over and over again, is the level of control over the magickal process that creating entities provides. This often leads to more favorable results in their workings and more workings in general.

Creating magickal entities can be as easy or as hard as you would like it to be. Even with the least amount of preparation, you can produce a "results focused" entity. Of course, the more that you put into your entity, the better your chances are of gaining the results that you desire.

Because of the flexibility inherent in their creation, magickal entities can be "custom designed" to a very specific goal. With some magickal workings, you are limited to the results produced. With an entity created specifically for your goal, you have better likelihood of the goal manifesting in the manner that you wish. Also, you have a better expectation of the results, whereas with other "generic" magickal workings the results gained may be close to what you had hoped for, but still not exactly as you had wanted or needed.

With some types of magickal workings, like sigils for example, you receive "Point A to Point B" type of results. In other words, there is little room for adding additional parameters into the magickal working once it has been enacted. With magickal entities on the other hand, you have the ability to redirect the entity's focus while the entity is actively working to produce your desired magickal results.

After creating the entity, little of your own energy is required to produce the results desired. Because of this, you are able to devote your time and energy to other things as you wish. The entity will go off and complete the task that has been assigned to it. The more energy that you direct toward your entity—depending on the work at hand—the better your results tend to be.

Expanding on the dynamic possibilities of entities, a magickal entity can be used for several magickal tasks at the same time. For example, an entity that has the task of creating wealth can be used to make a company prosperous. At the same time the entity can look after a person's personal assets. Often "general skilled" entities can be used over and over for magickal workings that are of similar basis. An example of this would be the creation of an entity that is governed by the realm of happiness. This entity could be used any time that a feeling of happiness was needed.

Magickal entities can be created to be "astral messengers." These messengers can go out and collect bits of information that is of interest to the creator. The entities then can report back to the creator relaying all of the information that was gathered. This type of entity use can be beneficial in times when someone needs to gather important information when under normal means it would be impossible, such as in making crucial business decisions.

An entity can be created to help you learn a specific skill. Often people will create what are often known as "teacher entities." These teacher entities are created with all of the knowledge of a particular skill or area of interest. The creator will then go to the entity to have it help teach the creator the desired skill or knowledge. Teacher entities are like having your very own wise mentor at your disposal. These types of entities can be very beneficial when trying to learn new and complicated subjects.

For some people, it is easier to use entities to bring on magickal results. One of the reasons for this is because when using other forms of magickal workings, it may be difficult to know how the desired event will manifest. This often leads to failed, half-realized workings, or workings that are not performed. When working with entities, the mage is able to relate to a "being" doing the working. For example, in protection workings, it is easier for most people to envision a big bloodthirsty beast ready to devour any and all that wish to cause the creator harm; rather than trying to envision a glowing light of energy keeping "wrong-doers" at bay.

In some magickal philosophies, magi are trained to never perform magick unless a real and needed result is desired. They are often taught to never use their magick on simple whims just to see if their magick works. This limitation often leads to poorly trained magi, as they are rarely able to practice what it is that they have learned. When the time comes to try to manifest something, they are often "rusty" or undereducated in certain magickal areas. When they try to put their skills to work, they often meet with poor results.

Some magi create magickal entities solely as means to hone their magickal abilities. By creating a magickal entity, they are putting many learned skills to work, while manifesting a real and needed result. The real and needed result is the creation of something that will allow them to expand their magickal abilities. Often these entities are dissolved soon after creation, as they serve no purposes other than to increase the mage's magickal aptitude. Some entities, however, are kept as a magickal companion much like a witch's familiar.

Magickal Entities can be used for finding rare books, for aiding in a job search, for helping sales of a product, for irritating an enemy, for protecting a house, etc. We have heard of magickal entities who help compress and expand time, assist in speedy passage through rush hour, and to ensure a business receives a payment for a product. Magickal entities are quite versatile.

Creating magickal entities can provide a lot of fun and excitement. The entity that you create is only limited by your imagination. For some, the simple knowledge that they are in control of an entity that they created can be the impetus for using this method of magickal working. Other people like knowing that they can be as creative as they wish to be. This is one form of magickal working that can be as exciting as the results that it produces.

# Attuning Your Energy

The first step to working with entities is learning to attune your energy to work with an entity. What that means is that you should have some degree of control over your own energy. If you do not, working with an entity, let alone creating one, may be difficult. What are some things that you can do to improve your connection with entities?

**Meditate**

Meditation is a tool that will allow you to gain control of your thoughts and actions. With proper control, anything is possible and accurate results can be achieved.

It is important to be clear in your mind what exactly it is that you want for your magickal working. Meditation will help you to define your goals and desires. It will also allow you to see the situation from different angles. This will often reveal hidden situations that may lend themselves to helping achieve your goals.

If you do not have a regular meditation routine, it is recommended that you start one as soon as possible. There are many books out on the subject. If you look in your local phone directory, you may be able to find local community classes that teach meditation.

You may even want to join a Tai Chi class if it is offered in your area. Tai Chi is a Chinese form of moving meditation. This serves you two-fold, as you gain the benefits of meditation as well as keeping your body fit and in tune with your spiritual growth.

**Exercise**

Regular exercise is an important factor in over-all health. Exercise not only will keep you in good physical shape, but also reduces stress, alleviates depression, and improves the quality of your sleep. You don't have to run out and get a membership at a gym. Try spending an hour doing martial arts, yoga, or any other type of exercise such as walking, dancing, swimming, or even inline skating. Exercise can aid you in daily attunement to your personal energy as well as the energies you work with. Physical exercise causes you to sweat, which helps clean some of the toxins out of your body. This will help your energy flow throughout your body better.

## Diet

A good diet and perhaps even a good multi-vitamin can make a big difference in your energy as well. There is no one "true" diet that everyone should follow. However, try to eat balanced meals with moderate portions. More small meals a day are sometimes better than three large meals a day. Buy or grow organic whenever you can and try to eat food that is minimally processed. Raw fruits and vegetables are more nutritious than when cooked. If you must cook them, steaming is preferred. If you're a meat-eater, organic meat and poultry or wild game is best. If you choose a vegetarian or vegan diet, make sure you get the protein and iron you need through nuts, seeds, tofu, etc. Drink lots of pure water. Cut back on caffeine, sugar, artificial colors and flavors, and preservatives. Changing your eating habits can be very difficult. You don't have to do it all at once, pick one or two of your unhealthy eating habits and replace them with new, healthy habits.

## Sleep

Getting enough sleep is very important for health and energy. With only a few exceptions, the average adult needs between 7 and 8 hours of sleep within each 24-hour period to be adequately alert for 16 to 17 hours. Without the proper amount of sleep, the body cannot and will not function to its fullest potential. If you have trouble sleeping, try taking a hot bath before you go to bed. Lavender and Chamomile are soothing scents...try spraying your sheets and pillow with water and a combination of lavender and chamomile essential oils. Don't drink caffeinated beverages or eat sugary foods before going to bed.

## Visualization

Another tool in your toolbox is the art of creative visualization. Creative visualization will help you align the physical, mental, and spiritual minds to act together to achieve a desired result. It also allows for you to gain insight and information that was once hidden. The type of information that you may receive may come in the form of a scent, an image in the mind's eye, a sense of coolness or warmth, etc.

Creative visualization is often thought of as a balancing act between meditation and hypnosis. This is because creative visualization has the controlled state of awareness that meditation affords. At the same time it has the potential "programming" power that hypnosis provides.

Self-help clinics and various magickal groups usually teach creative visualization. There are books that teach and explain the subject, but some individuals find it hard to practice creative visualization through the guidance of a book. Therefore it is recommended that you seek out a magickal group, self help group, or clinic that offers creative visualization courses. You may even want to supplement your practices and studies with some hypnosis training.

## Experiencing Energy Signatures

Each person and entity has their own energy signature. By learning to recognize your energy signature from someone else's, you become more attuned to the energy around you. There are many exercises that you can do to help you with this. One that is easy is making note of some of your friends' energy signatures (or how they feel to you when they are around you). When someone comes into a room where your back is to them, try and figure out who it is by their energy signature before turning around to see who it is. Of course, if you have friends that are magi, then you can structure this a bit more. Another way to attune yourself to someone's energy signature is to stand facing each other with your palms 1-2 inches apart from each other. Feel each other's energy and then decide who will be the leader. Now, the leader will move their hands around in circles, figure 8's, or whatever patterns they wish. The follower will follow their energy. Once you get used to this with your eyes open, both leader and follower should close their eyes and continue to follow the energy signature of their partner. Start slow at first, then speed things up, or start with your hands close together and then work them farther apart.

**Become More Creative**

Expanding your creativity is extremely helpful when working with any type of magick. When it comes to creating entities, however, creativity should be given the highest priority of development.

Thinking in a creative manner will allow you to solve a problem with at least ten different solutions, with most of them being highly feasible. When you think creatively, you realize that not only is anything possible, but that there may be several different ways to achieve success. Creative thinking allows you to see situations in a multidimensional aspect. This will allow you to find the fastest way to achieve results in a way that will make everyone involved satisfied with the outcome.

With a little bit of creative thinking, you may find solutions to your problems without the use of any magickal workings. When magick is required, however, your creative thinking skills will allow you to develop the best laid out plan of magickal attack, which will cover almost every area that needs to be addressed to assure a successful outcome for everyone and everything involved.

A method to start sharpening your creative thinking skills is to come up with ten solutions to every problem that you are faced with. The next time that you have an issue that needs to be resolved, write down on a piece of paper at least ten different possible ways to resolve the solution. You may at first get one or two with no problem, but when it comes to more than two you may find it difficult. If you do find it hard, that's OK, just keep thinking. Even if the idea sounds dumb or far-fetched write it down.

If you do this every time you have a situation to resolve, you will find that your ideas will become sharper and more focused than when you started this technique. The more that you use this creative thinking method, the more effective solutions you will come up with. You will come to notice that your thought process has changed and that you are starting to see opportunities where there were none before.

## Respect The Entities You Work With

When you start working with entities, of any type, always show the utmost respect for them. This is one thing that most people overlook when working with entities, man-made or preexisting. Many, either because of ill instruction or ignorance, try to dictate and control the entities through threats and intimidation. This is the surest way to minimize the effectiveness of your magickal workings.

To maximize your magickal workings, you should treat the entity as though it is a comrade or friend. When you work in this manner, the entity is more responsive to your wishes and will work harder to manifest your desires. It is similar to working with humans, the more you respect them and the better you treat them, the more that they will do for you.

Be aware that with any entity, created or not, trust goes both ways. You have to fulfill your end of the bargain even as it fulfills its end. If you don't, the repercussions are less than desirable. It's better to pay your dues when it is time than to let them grow beyond the means of payment. Your strength as a person and as a mage can sometimes be measured by how honorably you've conducted your affairs.

Of course there are exceptions to every rule. Like humans, some entities will not work any harder for you no matter how you treat them. In these instances, it is best to use your judgment as to whether you wish to continue to work with such an entity. After all, the entity was created by you to fulfill your desires, and if an entity shows any signs of not wishing to accomplish those goals, it is up to you to decide on what you wish to do about it.

Magick, in any form, requires energy to work. Only by actually doing magick on a daily basis, working with energy everyday, and learning to control energy, will your spiritual power grow stronger. You will become capable of using magick in a wide variety of ways, which includes creating and working with entities.

# Important Precautions

When working with entities, it is important to be aware of the consequences of this type of magickal working. Just like other forms of magickal workings, using entities comes with both responsibilities and cautions.

This section is not here to tell you what you should or should not do. It is here to make you aware of the things that you may encounter while working with entities, and things to think about when creating them. This section serves as a guide for you to fully think out what it is that you plan to do with your entity.

## Laws of Cause and Effect

In some religious and spiritual circles the "Law of Return" is a widely held and accepted doctrine. This "law" dictates that whatever action is done by you, you shall receive back. Therefore if you were to do good one day, you shall receive something good in return, and conversely if you do something bad, you shall receive something bad.

In Wicca they have something similar to the "Law of Return." They call this the "Three Fold Law." They understand this "law" to mean that what ever you do, good or bad, returns to you with three times the strength. There are differing views as to how and when you receive the three-fold effect, but nonetheless most Wiccans agree that such an effect occurs.

In some New Age groups the "Law of Return" is referred to as Karma (the force generated by a person's actions to perpetuate transmigration and in its ethical consequences to determine the nature of the person's next existence). Some even understand Karma to act as a cosmic score of "fate." In other words if Johnny does good, he will receive "x" amount of good Karma "points;" whereas if Sally does something bad, she will receive "x" amount of bad Karma "points." Then, depending on person's point of view in regards to Karma, these points will gather until the end of the person's life and they will either be "rewarded" with a better life in the next incarnation, or be "punished" with a worse one. Others believe that you receive these Karma "points" in this lifetime. Some refer to this line of thinking as "New Age Karma," or "Western Karma."

The classical understanding of Karma is said to mean "action." Action in the sense of how a ball falls to the ground after it has been thrown. Karma in this sense is a word of understanding cause and effect, rather than a system of punishment or reward. In this understanding, the punishment or reward comes from the person's ability to learn a lesson. For example, say Johnny were to touch an iron and as a result he burned his hand. The Karma in this example was the burned hand. Now if Johnny chooses to learn this lesson, and check to see if the iron is hot before touching it, he has been rewarded by not receiving a nasty burn as he had originally. On the other hand if he refuses to check the iron before he touches it, he is punished by receiving a burn the next time he touches a hot iron.

Regardless of what the system is named, "Law of Return," "Three Fold Law," Karma, etc., it is used to teach people the effect that their actions have. No matter how foolish some of these "laws" sound or are, the fundamental principle is to make the follower, student, mage, etc. learn to understand cause and effect.

It is of great importance to understand what type of effects your actions will have on the world around you. If you are careless, you may find that your actions can have an unexpected, ill effects on those that you love and care about. On the other hand, you may receive a great fortune by what seems to be luck.

Amanda created a magickal entity, which would slowly destroy a duplex. This entity also would torment the downstairs inhabitants as well as make the upstairs tenants uncomfortable in their surroundings, so much that they would want to move. Unfortunately, the next upstairs tenant was a good friend of Amanda's. One day when her friend was fixing the bathroom sink, it broke. Several days later, when he was fixing the kitchen sink, it also broke. A series of small mishaps at the duplex happened to this friend. She did not think out what would happen if a friend of hers ever would move in. This is an example of why it is important to think things through before creating an entity.

The reason for mentioning this here is to make you aware of how the planning and creation of your entity can affect things around you; for better or worse. We will not tell you that is bad, or bad things are going to happen to you, if you choose to have your entity cause harm or misfortune to someone. It is not for us to judge—that is up to you. However, you should completely think though all of the possible effects that your actions, and those of your entity, may have. Once you have thought through all of them, and are satisfied with all known possible results, only then should you proceed with your plans.

There are times when things may happen that you did not foresee. These are times to learn how your actions have caused an effect on something, and time to own up to your actions. If you learn from these incidents, you may be able to better plan your actions at a later time. Or you may be able to accept that there are some things that are outside of your ability to control at this time, and to take responsibility for them when they happen.

The primary thing that you should do is to plan your actions so that you will have no guilt when they are acted out. This will require you to think through everything. Think through to the future and try to foresee any problems that your actions may cause. See if you may have guilt in the future. If you are unable to see—honestly unable to see, and are not kidding yourself just to make something happen—only then should you proceed with your plans.

If you find that after your actions you do have guilt, the only thing that you should do is to correct the problem through whatever means possible. This may mean that you need to stop a magickal working that you have done. This may even mean that you just have to accept what has happened and move on with your life. But whatever it is that you need to do, do it and take full responsibility of your actions.

One last note about cause and effect: what ever your entity does, it does because of you and your intentions. Therefore do not fall into the false security of kidding yourself by saying that since your entity did it and you did not, you are not responsible for what happened.

## Dependence on Entity Use

Sometimes when we use things, we begin to incorporate them into our lives. Soon we find it hard to think of a time when we didn't use such an item. We find ourselves dependent on that item.

The same can be true when we start to work with the entities that we create (and even the ones that we don't). Of course, depending on the level of dependency, this may not necessarily be a bad thing. We have dependencies with all kinds of things in our lives, and without them we may have to function  differently, and it may take us longer, but we are still able to function. The dependencies that may develop through working with entities may only reach that level.

When we come to depend on entities more than most other things, we may be putting ourselves into the path of problems. Some people create entities that do things like inspire creative thought or allow the picking of a winning horse. For a writer, if the entity of creative inspiration were to not work for some reason, after a long time of reliable service, the writer may find him or herself in a real predicament. The person that make his or her "luxury" income through the earnings on horse betting, may soon find themselves with a real problem when they start losing money as opposed to making it. There is nothing wrong with having a "mild" dependency on an entity that you create, as long as you are still able to function in a normally without that entity.

When you create an entity, do so with the under-standing that the entity is only here to help. The entity is not here to do everything for you. If you follow this rule of thumb, you should not experience any negative issues when working with the entity that you create.

# GOALS AND RESULTS

What is it that I want the entity to do? How will the entity accomplish this task? What variables do I need to factor in so that the entity is successful? What is my timetable? How do I insure that the entity is doing its task? How do I wish the entity to appear to me?

These questions as well as others are important questions to ask and answer. Take time to develop your answers, be sure of exactly what it is you want to do with the entity and make sure you impress that into the entity. These questions will help you focus and attune your energy toward achieving what you want with the entity and will also insure that the experience is well worth the time invested.

An important question to ask yourself is the following: Is it worth it to conjure the entity and have it do the task or are there other means to achieve my ends? Now it may seem odd to ask this question in this book, but it is a very important and valid question to ask. It is not to say you shouldn't create entities, but you should be certain that it is justified. If you are one who likes to experiment, then your justification is just that—in order to learn more about entities, you work with them. By asking and answering this question, you will insure yourself no regret, but rather, a focused intent that will bring about what you want in a manner that works for you. Any magickal undertaking should be considered carefully and entity work is no exception.

Picture in your minds eye exactly what it is that you want. Try to see your desire manifested. See everything that would be affected by it. How would you feel? What problems would this solve for you? How would it make other people feel? Try to make the desire manifestation as real as possible. Try to understand the feelings that you would have once it has come to pass.

After you have crystallized your desire as much as possible, for every conceivable aspect, write it down in as much detail as you can. Write down the results that you will achieve from the desire. Write your emotions and feelings in regards to the desire that will manifest. Capture the essence of what this desire will bring into your life. Make this as clear and as detailed as possible.

When you have written all of this down, you have taken your first step toward manifesting your desires. In many magickal systems, writing down the desire in as much detail creates an astral "blueprint" for your goals. This "blueprint" is the starting point for all things to come into being.

One you are finished writing down everything that you can think of, determine from what source your desire will come, and the impact that the source may have. In other words, if your desire was to receive a lump some of money (yes, the standard "magickal how-to" example), where would the money come from? Would you receive it through the means of payment for an art sculpture that you have recently finished? Would you find an envelope full of money on your way to the park? Will the money come from a disability settlement from the accident at work that left you without the use of your right arm? Did you receive it because a dear person to you died and stated in his or her will that you are to receive the money?

As you can see, there are many ways that you could receive the lump sum of cash in a favorable way. You can also see that there are numerous ways to gain the money that you may not like—like losing your arm, or the death of a loved one. The purpose of this exercise is so that you can try to find the best, and second best, possible ways for you to have your goal manifest. By doing this, you are trying to eliminate, to the best of your ability, any "negative" source that you would not want your desire to manifest through.

When you have found the best ways for your desire to come into being, write it down. Then visualize your receiving your desire through the source(s) that you have chosen. Does it feel right to you? Have you thought of everything that may come from this source? If you can honestly say "yes," then that is the most logical source for you. If you answered "no," then keep thinking of a better source until you have found one that works for you.

Now you should put the paper a way for a day or two and try not to think about your desire. It may be hard not to, but do the best that you can. If you find yourself thinking about it, acknowledge it for what it is and allow it to pass.

What this will do, is allow your subconscious to figure out the easiest and best way to manifest your desires, within the frame work that you have provided. It will mull over the details that you may not have thought about. It will then decide if it is able to do it or not.

In some cases, your subconscious may need more details. It may even suggest a different route to gain the desires. All of this will help to lead you to the manifestation of your desires. This is called the "incubation stage."

After a day or two of allowing your subconscious to build a plan, take out the paper and review what was written down. Does what you have written still make sense to you? Is this still what you want? You may find that what was written is still exactly what you want. You may also find that you want to add or subtract a few things, but that over all the idea is sound.

Still you may find that you were going about obtaining the desire the wrong way. You may now have fresh new ideas to try out that will better your chances at attaining your goals. Others will find that, after taking time out to "incubate" their thoughts, their written desires really are not what they truly want. New ideas and thoughts may come to the surface.

Continue to develop your magickal goals and desires until you are honestly happy with what you have. It is then that you can begin to design an entity to bring your desires and goals into manifestation.

We mentioned the need to define possible results and outcomes from using the entity. This does not mean you should lust for results, i.e. expect that a result will occur instantaneously and that your problem will be solved. This is not to say that you should not think about it, just don't think about the results all the time. This may cause you to be disappointed when the results you expect don't happen. Magick is a subtle force and shows itself in subtle ways. When working with an entity, you should certainly have an idea of what kind of result will come about through the use of the entity. Just don't let that result become an obsession. Further, recognize variations of the result you wanted. Sometimes you won't quite accomplish what you set out to do, but the result can still be useful to you.

# Planning Your Entity

Now that you have defined your goals and desires, it is time to define the purpose(s) of your entity. It is time to think about the task(s) of the entity. Think about the role it will play in the manifestation of your goals and desires.

In the example provided earlier, the attainment of a lump some of cash, your entity could have different types of tasks based upon your goals and desires. Let's say for example that you wish to receive a lump sum of cash, and you wish to receive it through the sale of a sculpture. You may wish to have the entity provide inspiration and fine craftsmanship to you during the creation of the sculpture. You may wish to have the entity attract the attention of fine art collectors from your region to buy your artwork. Then entity could even have a task of influencing anyone that lays eyes upon the artwork to want to buy the piece. There are many options available to you during the creation of your entity's task(s).

After you have defined the entity's task(s), you must figure out the realm of influence the entity will have. The realm of influence is like the "trade" or "craft" of the entity. There are two realms of influence that need to be defined, the general and the specific.

The general realm of influence describes what type of "trade" or "craft" the entity is involved in. For example a baseball player would have the general realm of influence in sports. A journalist could have different ones to choose from—depending on the way you want to look at it. The journalist's general realm of influence could be information or art (assuming that you view writing as an art-form).

In the "lump sum of cash" entity example from above, you have decided to make the entity's task to influence people to buy your sculpture. You can then look at the task and decide that the entity's general realm of influence is "sales." This would mean that the entity is knowledgeable in the art of selling things. Once you have the general realm of influence, you can use that information to think about and gather correspondence ideas for later incorporation with the entity.

For the "lump sum of cash" entity, with a general realm of influence in "sales," you may start thinking of things, like orange—for attraction, rose pedals—for love or admiration, etc. These ideas will be things that you can, and should, use when creating your entity. Later we will discuss how to incorporate these ideas into your entity.

After you have figured out the general realm of intent, it is time to create the specific realm of influence. Going back to our baseball player example, his or her specific realm of intent may be "the pitcher for the New York City Screaming Eagles." The journalist's specific realm of influence could be "star reporter for the Orlando Music Press."

The "lump sum of cash" entity could have a specific realm of influence of "attractor of and seller to purchasers of fine art." Armed with the specific realm of influence, we are able to start to develop the entity's statement of intent, which will become the core—or DNA, if you will—of the entity. The statement of intent for this entity could be "To influence and attract fine art purchasers that are willing and able to purchase my sculpture for price that I set."

Now you have the core of the entity's existence defined. This will make it much easier for you to create your entity. It will also improve the likelihood that your magickal working will produce the results that you wish to attain.

Perform divination to make sure that the entity's purpose is for the best of all that it will have an effect over. In other words, you want to make sure that the purpose of the entity is sound and correct with your ethical principals and will not cause any adverse effects that you may have not thought of.

Be honest with yourself when divining, because it can be very tempting to make yourself believe that a reading is telling you to proceed, even though the reading is trying to issue to you a dire warning. You may want to enlist the help of a trusted person to perform the divination for you. Having the "outside" person perform a reading for you may be the buffer that you need to make sure that you are engaging in a magickal working that is truly in your best interest.

If the divination reading turns out to not be in your best interest, all is not lost. It is best to take the recommendations from the reading and try looking at your goals and desires for hidden ideas. You may want to sleep on it before reviewing your goals. This will bring upon the "incubation" again to help you clear out unwanted influences.

After you have had time to review, it's time to start over. Look for areas that you may have missed the first time. Look for things that the reading suggested to be changed. After all of this, it is time to go back to divination to see if your new plan is beneficial to you.

Once you get a "go ahead" reading, you should continue with the creation of your entity. It should be fairly easy from here on out.

# CHOOSING A NAME

Naming an entity can be one of the most difficult things to do for some magi. Some, unnecessarily, agonize over what type of name would give justice to their creation. Others are afraid that they are not creative enough to come up with an original name. Still others fear that the name that they pick will conflict with preexisting entities.

For most, however, naming an entity is just as easy as breathing. There really is no reason why you should feel any differently about the subject. There are many different formulas and methods that you can employ to help you come up with a name that suits your entity.

One of the easiest ways of naming an entity is to derive its name from the statement of intent. This is done by first taking the statement of intent, "To influence and attract fine art purchasers that are able to and that will purchase my sculpture for price that I set," for example, and removing all of the unneeded words like "a," "the," "and," "that," "of," etc. Ideally you should have around three to nine words left, for example "influence attract fine art purchasers able will purchase my sculpture price I set." As you can see from the example, the "three to nine words left" rule of thumb will not be valid in every case.

Next you will take the first letter of the remaining words, and combine those letters together to form the entity's name. So in our example, we would have "iafarawpmspis." As you can see, this name is very unintelligible and not easily pronounceable. In this case we will further reduce the name down by removing all of the repeated letters. When we do this, we come up with "iafrwpms."

The result is somewhat more manageable, but lacking some vowels, it is still difficult to work with. In such cases, we will want to add vowels that will allow for us to create a name that is pronounceable. Choosing the extra letters can be done in many different fashions. One of the easiest is to pick and choose the letters that you think will compliment the name the best. Another way is to choose the letters that have numerical symbolism that will bring the full name to a number, via numerology, that resonates with the entity's task. For our example, we will take the numerology route, which gives us "firiwaspim" with a numerology equivalent of the number 6 (magnetic, sociable, artistic, etc.) using the Pythagorean system of numerology. Now this is a little bit easier to read and say, but we are going to take it a bit further and split the name into two. Doing that gives us "Firi Waspim."

Sometimes you may want to name the entity after it's function, like "buy new car." You may want to spell it backwards like "rac wen yub," and combine them to form the name of "Racwenyub." The names may be long, or unpronounceable in the long form. If this is the case, it is OK to break the name up like "Racwen Yub," or "Rac Yubwen."

The reason for spelling the words backward is to free your mind of the name's meaning and also to give the feeling of "antiquated" names of spirits of old often found in spell books and such—this is not necessary, it is merely a point of personal taste. Some magi feel that working with entities with "odd" names seem to help them in focusing on the magickal working at hand, while others feel that it hinders them. Use what feels and works best for you.

What ever type of naming convention you use, it is a good idea to try, if possible, to somehow incorporate the entity's task into the name. This will serve to further the entity's connection to the desired task and will build power in the use of the entity.

One thing that should be mentioned here, is that you should be wary of any negative feelings that you get from a name, whether you constructed the name from scratch or simply chose describing words. If the name feels negative to you, or has negative descriptive words, it may hinder your magickal workings. This is not to say if you are constructing an entity to curse someone or thing that it should not sound negative in general, rather the name should not feel negative to you—the one working with it. If it does feel negative to you, in other words you don't like the name or it leaves a bad feeling when saying or working with it, then you should not use it. For if you do, you may begin to resent your entity, and your magickal working may not manifest in the manner in which you had hoped. Always try to name your entity with a name that you like and that feels good to you when you work with it.

Of course you do not have to name your entity at all. Some very successful entities have never been named. Naming them, however affords them personality. Since we, as humans, tend to have an easier time relating to things that have names.

Names also allow us to have control over that which is named. In some magickal traditions, names are symbolic of the thing that is named. Because of this, by naming a thing—or entity in this case—you can guide it to do your wishes. That is an important thing to keep in mind when creating your entity—after all, you are creating it to serve you and your wishes.

# Your Entity's Appearance

There are many different ways to come up with an appearance for your entity. A rather simple way is to take its general realm of influence and look for symbolism that would afford a good appearance. You could also think about the entity's task and then design an appearance that would be best suited for completing the task successfully. The list is seemingly endless.

We will focus on a method that is not well documented on general occult circles. This method creates the entity's appearance from the letters of its name. You do this by taking the name and turning the letters into symbolic representations of the astral body parts of the entity. The first letter represents the head area, and the last letter represents its foot area. The remaining letters represent different parts between the head and foot regions. The amount of detail depends on the amount of letters that are between the first and last letters—the more letters the finer the details, the fewer letters the more general the details.

In our example, we will use numerology as our symbolism. In numerology, specifically Pythagorean numerology, each number is assigned to a letter of the alphabet and is viewed as feminine or masculine. Every number has a specific "characteristic" which can lend to us an idea of what the entity can look like.

Our example entity, Firi Waspim, has the letter "F" as a head and the letter "M" as the feet. So, looking to our numerology, we see that the letter "F" is the number six. The number six, which is feminine in nature, will provide our entity with female-like features in the face. Since the number six is associated with occupations like artists, host/hostess, advisers, public speakers, etc. we can start to visualize the facial features of people that fill those roles. The letter "M" is also feminine by nature due to its association with the number four. The number four is related to the occupations of architect, sculptor, TV or radio personality, etc.

We will continue to do this for the rest of the letters in the entity's name. You will find that in numerology a number can represent different many different things. It is up to you to decide which aspect  that you wish to have associated with your entity. For  example, we have chosen the following associations for our example entity:

| | | |
|---|---|---|
| F: | Head | 6 (Feminine)—Adviser |
| I: | Neck | 9 (Masculine)—Artist |
| R: | Upper Chest | 9 (Masculine)—Artist |
| I: | Arms/Hands | 9 (Masculine)—Artist |
| W: | Lower Chest | 5 (Masculine)—Salesperson |
| A: | Stomach | 1 (Masculine)—Expert |
| S: | Buttocks Area | 1 (Masculine)—Expert |
| P: | Thighs | 7 (Masculine)—Poet |
| I: | Shin Area | 9 (Masculine)—Artist |
| M: | Feet | 4 (Feminine)—Sculpture |

We have chosen professions that we feel will add to the entity persona, and provide us with an idea of what it should look like. We can also look at the amount of feminine and masculine letters/numbers that make up the name to find out its sex. In our example we have a greater number of masculine letters/numbers than feminine letters/numbers, so our entity is male.

You can use any system that you feel comfortable with to use as the symbolism for the letters. For example a mage that is versed in Norse Mythology may want to use some incarnation of Runes. Another mage, knowledgeable in the Kabbalah, may wish to use the Hebraic alphabet to aid in his or her creation of his or her entity's appearance. The important thing is to use what ever feels right to you, and works best for you.

Even though our example suggests that our entity is anthropomorphic, this does not have to be the case. In many books entities often take on shapes that are not found in our common everyday lives. Some of these entities were half beast or half animal. Other entities were completely alien in appearance. You may create your entity's appearance in any form or fashion that you would like. An important thing to remember, besides doing what feels right and works best for you, is to make sure that the appearance of your entity is in harmony with its realms of influence. It would be counter productive to have an entity that beautifies things to look so horrible that you could not stand to look at it.

Unless you have a specific reason not to, you should try to keep your entity's appearance related to its task(s). Think of it like this, lets say you took your car to an auto-mechanic's shop. You notice that all of the mechanics are wearing three-piece suits. You also notice that this is not the first time that they have worn these suits—they wear them all of the time. There is never a spec or spot on them. Would you feel comfortable taking your car to this shop? What kind of work could you expect from it? There is nothing saying that this may not be the best shop in the world, but by going on looks alone, you may have reservations about having your car worked on there. This is something that you should think about when constructing your entity's appearance. You should make sure that you are satisfied with the appearance of your entity and that it is right for its task(s). This will make it easier for you to do the magickal working at hand.

# Housing Your Entity

One of the easiest ways for people to interact with entities is to evoke the entity into a physical item. Usually the physical containers of entities resemble the entities themselves. It is thought that as long as the physical container resembles the entity as much as possible, the entity will feel encouraged to stay in its physical representation.

Using objects as the physical bodies of entities is very effective for magickal workings, because it calls upon the instinctive and intuitive behaviors from our childhood. Children are born with the ability to give life to things. An example of this is the ability to give life to their toys; they are so good at this that they even have the ability to hear them speak. The way that a child creates an imaginary friend is similar to the manner in which you would create an entity.

Using images as a focal point of entity communication is nothing new. Catholics pray to Saints, Jesus, Mary, etc. by using paintings, statues, and altars to aid their communication. This technique of working with entities has been used for thousands of years by many different cultures.

Making a physical object have an entity live within it can be as simple or complex as you want it to be. The basic requirement to animate an object is to treat it as though it were already alive. Once this basic requirement has been understood, it can be dressed up as fancily as you would like, though you are not required to do so. Because of its ease, many people may not acknowledge its effectiveness.

The technique noted above is very similar to the way witches create familiars. Alchemists have used the technique to impregnate their formulas with entities. This technique has been able to remain "occult" (i.e., hidden or secret) due to its simplicity. It is a classic case of hiding something in plain sight. It has been disregard because of its simplicity, and thus remains a very effective and powerful occult technique.

What attracts entities to take up residence in physical objects is the sincerity and devotion of a person wishing to have such an entity. The person, of course, must have firm faith and belief in the presence of the entity. Ritual, to create an entity or otherwise, helps to express this sincerity and devotion. Rituals can also be used to confirm the person's faith in the entity.

Entities respond very well to the idea of "like attracts like" (i.e., that the more two things resemble each other, the more likely they are to relate to one another). Having understood this, it becomes very important to carefully choose the symbols and characteristics of the physical object within which you wish your entity to reside.

Nearly anything can serve to house an entity. If you can identify it, it can be a suitable home for an entity, although some objects are better than others. Objects that are harmonious with the entity's realm of influence are a better choice than those that are not.

The size of the entity's home is not of great importance. What really matters is the shape, appearance, and the substance of the home. The object should be of a size that is convenient to work with.

When selecting a suitable home for your entity, you have two choices. The first choice is to select a prefabricated object. This can range from statues of all shapes, sizes, and substances to pictures, paintings, candles, rocks, buildings, balloons, books, glasses, computers, animals, plants, talismans, dolls, telephones, crystals, or even a remittance envelope for your business bearing your entity's programming symbol on it. The second option is to construct the housing using your knowledge of the entity's personality, realm of influence, and other occult virtues.

Whatever the object is, it must be one that is attractive to you. It must stir feelings of interest. If the housing seems lifeless or uninteresting, it will be a poor home for the entity. To be effective, the housing must have qualities that make you want to interact with it.

It is better to avoid objects that resemble a living or dead person that you know in any fashion or recognize. This will help you keep your work with your entity as pure as possible. If such objects are used, you may confuse the energy of the person with that of the entity. This may cause ill effects on the person that the object resembles. Of course this does not apply if you are intentionally trying to create an entity that is to have a bond with the person represented by the object.

Entity housing can be formed from just about anything. The important thing to remember is to choose materials that will withstand wear, tear, and repeated handling for the life of the entity.

Taylor has entities that are housed within his voice, coming forth only when he says specific words, while others go into a more sight oriented manifestation, like his paintings. Amanda's Faerie Thought-Forms (e.g. Faerie of Lost Things, Faerie of Sweet Dreams, etc.) are housed within various faerie statues. She has also housed a vengeance entity within a house itself. David houses entities in bottles, candles, keys, and even an arrowhead. Usually the housing is chosen out of convenience rather than symbolism. Be creative when creating the appearance and housing of the entity. After all, the appearance can be descriptive of what the entity is and what it does.

If you are artistic, you may want to create the object yourself. By doing so, you are unconsciously forming the entity in your mind. This will serve to strengthen the bond between the entity and youself. Also, in this way the object will resonate deep within your psyche and improve your workings with the entity.

When creating an object for the entity to live in, you may want to plan for a cavity in the object that will allow for you to deposit items vital to the entity. For example, you may want to place the entity's task and programming symbol on a small scroll and place it inside the cavity. You may want to have an area that you can place blood, semen, or other fluids during the ritual giving life to the entity. There are many other reasons, if you choose to have one, for leaving a cavity in the entity's housing.

If you are constructing the entity's housing, you may wish to incorporate a color, or colors, that correspond and are harmonious to the entity's realm of influence. If you are not sure which color or colors to use, choose something that is attractive and pleasing to you.

You may also wish to use astrological times when creating the entity's housing. Magickal workings can be greatly influenced if they are used. On the other hand, it is not essential to use them either. As a matter of fact, the magickal working can be greatly simplified if they are not used. It can be helpful, however, to do workings during the proper phase of the moon, and on days that are harmonious with your magickal endeavor.

In ancient times people would use stones and crystals, with appropriate attributes, to bind an entity to a plant that had similar attributes to the entity's realm of influence. As long as the plant and stones were harmonious with the entity, it would use the plant as a home while working with the person that bound it. The stones served to charge the plant with the energy of the entity and with its realm of influence. If you have a green thumb and a bit of ingenuity and creativity, you could do something similar.

Once an entity has been provided with a physical body, it tends to respond and perform better than a disembodied one. Also, an entity with a physical body tends to show more interest in human experience. Therefore, an embodied entity will actually want to help you in your efforts. This will provide the entity the human experiences that it soon grows accustom to.

Not all entities require housings. Short-term entities sometimes have a life span that is so short that a physical housing is not necessary. For those types of entities, it may be better to link (or "house") them to aromas. The aroma could be inhaled during the creation and evocation of your entity. You may even wish to anoint a physical housing, if one is used, with the selected aroma. Remember to choose one that that is appealing to you and is harmonious with the entity's realm of influence.

You may want to consider constructing a shrine for the entity. The entity's housing serves as the "physical body" of the entity, while the shrine serves as the "house" of the entity. The shrine does not need to be detailed or elaborate. Again, the most important things to remember are to make sure that it is pleasing and attractive to you, and that it fits the personality of the entity and its realm of influence. You may even wish to make your shrine "portable." This will allow you to move it, or keep it out of sight.

Whenever you attempt to create an entity, the physical object in which it is to reside, or both, use personal judgment and intuition. There are many correspondences with specific meanings and uses in most, if not all, magickal systems. Because of this, it may be difficult to decide which one to use. If you have a general idea of what the entity's realm of influence is, this will help narrow down the choices that you have. In any rate, use your own mind to guide you and never act as a slave to any magickal system.

# FEEDING TIME

Energy of some form or another has to be supplied in order for an entity to exist. Entities feed off energy, much like we eat and drink. Just as you would die if you didn't eat, so too will an entity cease to exist without proper energy. Therefore when creating an entity, great consideration must be taken as to where and how the entity will receive its regular supply of energy.

Feeding the entity need not be too difficult. There are two common ways that the entity can receive energy. The first is to feed an entity from your personal energy, and the second is to have it feed from and energy source external to you.

When you first create an entity, an amount of your energy is used to give the entity life. You can continue to be the entity's sole source of energy if you would like to have an entity totally dependent on you for its existence. The way that you could "feed" your entity energy from you is to talk to it daily. This will help to build the connection between you and your entity, while at the same time directing your personal attention and energy to it from which it can feed. Another way is to offer it devotional plates of food. Of course the entity will not eat the physical food, rather it will feed off of the essence of the food. This act is a sign of your affection. You can also meditate on the image of the entity and visualize energy streaming from your astral body and flowing into that of the entity. Basically any attention that you give to the entity can serve as an "energy feeding." There are many other ways to accomplish this if you take the time to find what is right for you and to allow yourself to be creative.

Just as there are many ways to creatively feed your entity energy from yourself, there are as many ways to creatively feed the entity from an energy source external to you. If your entity's task is to help dissolve automobile traffic jams and things of the like, you could assign the entity to feed off of the energy patterns generated from automobile traffic. By doing this you have eliminated the need for constant attention from you in order for the entity to survive, and you have provided it with a relatively endless supply of energy—provided that there is always automobile traffic. Any time that you would call upon the entity to help you out in a traffic jam, your added attention and energy would help to boost the entity's ability to do its job.

If you were to create an entity to help you out with homework, you could assign the entity to feed off of the very source that creates the homework. By doing that, you have an entity that will always have a supply of energy to help you with your homework as long as there is homework to do. What happens if there is no more homework and your entity starves? That is fine, because as long as there is no homework, you have no need of an entity to help you with homework. Therefore, the "homework entity" will just fade from existence.

You can also create a hybrid system of feeding your entity. You can make it so that the entity has a constant source of energy external to you, but when you feed it energy—through whatever means—the entity receives a great energy boost. That energy boost can be used to help you (or what ever the entity is created to do) much more efficiently. Also by specifying a secondary form of energy external to you, you ensure the entity's existence during those times that you do not actively need its services. It is kind of like a child that learns that it can eat food outside of its home to survive, but seems to enjoy and benefit from home-cooked meals more.

Whatever energy source that you provide to your entity, there are two things to keep in mind. The first thing is to make sure that the source of energy is harmonious with the task and the realm of influence of the entity, and that the source of energy is pleasing to you (because if it is not pleasing, or becomes a burden on you to provide, your entity will suffer from it). The second thing to remember is to make sure that you give your entity some form of energy and that your entity knows where its next meal is coming from. If you forget to do this, your entity may never come into existence, or (as some occultists seem to believe) your entity could become a roaming "vampire" looking for energy wherever it may find it.

# MAGICKAL ABILITIES

To create an entity you need to know what types of abilities it should have. What types of qualities should your entity have? Since you already have decided on the entity's realm of influence and its appearance, you should think about what types of tools—if any at all—it uses and if it wears anything special like a cloak, ring, or necklace to help it in achieving its task(s).

For those of you that may be creating an entity that will last a while or for those of you that like writing and being creative, you may benefit from writing a short biography of your entity's magickal abilities. This biography should detail how great the entity is at its magickal task. You can describe how your entity reacts to different situations, how it solves specific problems, how it interacts with people and animals, etc. Try to give as much life to your entity as you can through your details.

After you have finished writing the entity's magickal biography, you should read it. Make sure that every little detail of the biography is firmly planted into your memory. After it is etched deep within your psyche, let it work in your mind for a day or two. You may even wish to let it work in your subconscious for up to a week for better results. During this time of incubation, your subconscious builds up the details needed to construct this entity.

After this time has elapsed and you return to work on your entity, you may find that your subconscious has, partially, if not completely, finished the description of your entity's magickal abilities. Then when you do any working on or with your entity, you will find that things manifest and work more smoothly than they would have otherwise.

Even if you do not write a biography for your entity, it is important to at least think about your entity's magickal abilities. Plan out the ways that your entity deals with things specific to its task(s). This will help you to firmly understand your entity and make working with it that much easier.

# LIFE SPAN

One thing that most people seem to ignore when creating
entities is the duration of life that the entity shall have.
Therefore to avoid any unforeseen problems or issues that
may arise due to your entity not having a defined term
of life, you should consider the life span of the entity. The
reasons to disperse an entity can be varied. The entity may
have completed its task or it may not be doing its task. You
may feel that you can handle the task on your own and no
longer need the entity. Whatever the reason, as long as you
follow through with it, you know you are not dependant
on the entity.

By defining your entity's life span, you are taking
responsibility for your actions. It also provides closure for
you in regards to the entity and its task. Understanding the
life span of the entity helps to put the things of the past into
the past. It allows you to have a clear vision of the present
and the future.

In order to determine the life span of the entity, we
should look at its purpose. What is the entity supposed to
do? Was it created for a one-time event, or was it created
to work with an ongoing issue? Do you want the entity
to continue to live after that specific task was completed,
because you know that more of the same type of tasks will
arise later in life? Would you rather have this entity's existence halt with the completion of its task; and if the same
tasks happen later in life, build a better entity using the
lessons that you have learned from original experience? Do
you want the entity to terminate by a specific point in time
regardless if the task has been completed or not? These are

all things that you may want to consider when thinking about the life span for your entity.

Once you have figured out what the life span of your entity will be, you may want to think of different time references to use as your marker of time. For example you may wish to have the entity only active during the waxing moon and terminate on the third full moon after the entity's creation. You could have the entity's life cease on the Monday immediately after the entity's task has been completed.

An even easier way to determine the entity's life is to directly add it to the statement of intent. An example of this could be: Provide me with the best opportunity for financial security that is in alignment with my goals, dreams, and desires, after doing so your service to me will end and you shall exist no more.

If the entity is to last a lifetime, you may wish to have the entity terminate it's life when your life ceases. Even if your entity is to last forever, it is a good idea to solidify that in some form or fashion. This will make your entity have more definition to its existence and allow for you to work with it in a more meaningful manner.

Another thing to consider, along with the life span, is the manner in which the entity will be dissolved; assuming, of course, that the entity will have a finite existence. This also adds to the physiological aspect of providing closure.

Some people chose to destroy the entity's housing at the set time of dissolution. Others like to bury the housing. Others like to visualize the entity dissipating into the astral plane leaving its housing an empty shell of what used to be. Some just throw anything associated to the entity into the garbage. Some pull out the essential energy that they've put into the entity, which came from themselves initially. They destroy the link between the entity and themselves by visualizing the entity's energy coming back into them.

Most people find this easy since each person has their own unique energy signature. Calling that energy back to yourself is simply a matter of being attuned to it. You should, if you so choose, come up some form of dissolution for your entity when the time comes for it to cease. Most agree, when you terminate the life of an entity, you must handle this personally, either through absorption of energy or within the statement of intent.

Of course this is not applicable for those entities with perpetual life. However, you may still wish to decide on some form of dissolution just in case you, or anyone else that you allow to, wishes to have the entity cease existence. Usually people that have perpetual entities will put in a dissolution clause into the creation of the entity just in case the entity—for whatever reason—does not act according to plan. This is a smart thing to consider if you do decide to create a perpetual entity.

# Programming Your Intent

Some say, and we agree, that symbols are the language of the deep mind. Dreams are an example of this deep mind language communication. Humans react and relate to symbols more easily and rapidly then they do to the written or spoken word. This is because our subconscious communicates through a specialized form of symbolic language. Thus, using symbols allows us to communicate with our own and others' deep subconscious minds more effectively than most other modes of communication.

Symbols can take the form of any medium that stands for or suggests something else. For example, the lion is often used to represent courage. Symbols can also be objects, sounds, colors, aromas, or actions representing something to the unconscious mind, and having subjective cultural significance and the capacity to excite or objectify a response.

There are many different types of symbols to choose from. The symbols that have been constructed from your subconscious will prove to be more "powerful" than any other symbols that you may choose to use. This is because such symbols speak directly to your subconscious, as they were formed and created there. For example an image of a cat to one person may bring on thoughts and feelings of love and caring, while for another person it may bring thoughts of rejection and aggression. These thoughts and ideas were constructed from each person's subconscious through the experiences that they have had with cats. The first person may have only had great experiences with cats that were cuddly and loving, whereas the other person may have only experienced cats that wanted nothing to do with people and other cats that liked to scratch people. Such symbolic relationships are more powerful for these people because they have been constructed in their subconscious and then externalized into the form "cat."

To help define the core essence, or DNA if you will, of the entity, it is often a good idea to formulate symbols to represent the entity's realms (general and specific) of influence, its magickal abilities, life span, its statement of intent, its specific task(s), etc. Use only those things that you feel are most important to this entity. Then creatively find a way to combine them or incorporate them into one symbol representing the over all objective of the entity. Doing this will communicate and solidify, within your subconscious, the entity that you are choosing to manifest. This is known as programming your intent.

Of course it is important for you to choose a system or method for finding or creating symbols that you are comfortable with and that are effective for you. When you have created the *programming symbol*, you may want to incorporate it into the entity's housing. You can paint it on, carve it, glue a picture of it on the housing, etc. Of course this is entirely up to you to decide if you even want to do include it into the housing. Though, it is always a good idea to create a programming symbol, even if you choose not to incorporate it into the housing.

Programming Symbol
for
House Protection Entity

**House**

**Beth**
House

**Delta**
Fourfold/
Elements

**Thorn**
Protection

**Sun/Circle**
Balance/Solidity

**Moon**
Protection

# GIVING LIFE TO YOUR ENTITY

After you have finished with all of the details for your entity, it is time to bring it to life and send it on its way to manifest your desires. There are many ways to give life to your entity. We will outline a simple method and provide suggestions that you may want to expand upon.

**The Basic Entity Creation Sequence:**

> 1. Cleansing and Balancing
> 2. Statement of Magickal Intent
> 3. Alignment of Desire and Charging of Entity
> 4. Closing

**Cleansing and Balancing**

It is a good idea to physically clean the area before you work in it. The same is true with you; you may wish to take a bath or shower beforehand, as this will subconsciously show your dedication and sincerity to the working. Set up the room in which you will perform this working as you would for any other working.

Music can be helpful to charging an object with a magickal intent. The music helps to set the mood; while at the same time provides an intended distraction to help with the working. As long as the type of music is suited for the type of magickal working, it will fill your ears with sound. This will help to allow the mind to focus on the task at hand. If no music is present, your mind may have to work harder not to be distracted and to focus on the task.

Place all of the items related to the entity (housing object, programming symbol, shrine, etc.) in front of you and individually cleanse each item in the form or fashion that you are comfortable with. Alternatively, you can wave the smoke of incense or smudge over the objects to cleanse them that way. This is entirely up to you.

You should use a balancing (or banishing as some occultists refer to it as) ritual that you are familiar and comfortable with and that is best suited to your magickal system. You may wish to use the Opening of the Watchtower, or something similar, at this point. If you don't know any balancing (banishing) rituals, you can look in books, search on-line, etc for some ideas. The most effective balancing rituals, like all others, are the ones that you personally write.

## Statement of Magickal Intent

This is simply you stating to the forces that be your intent to create an entity to manifest your desires. A simple statement of intent for the magickal working could be: "It is my will and desire to create and give life to the entity (entity's name here) to go forth and (the entity's task). As it is my will, so it is done."

## Alignment of Desire and Charging Entity

This is where you energize and charge yourself and the area that you are working in with your desire. This step usually includes controlled breathing, visualization, meditation, etc. If you do not have a favorite way of doing this, the middle pillar exercise, or something similar, would be appropriate.

This is also where you will charge the entity, and anything that is to be related to the entity, with life. Any rite that you normally use to charge spells and/or other magickal workings can be used to charge an entity. Instruct the entity when, where, how, and for how long it will work. Instruct it how it will receive energy to live, that it should return to its housing object (if one is used) when it is not working (if you so desire it to), etc. Instruct it in how its existence will terminate. We have provided some suggestions for charging the entity below.

One way to charge yourself with the essence of the entity is to gaze upon the programming symbol and visualize the task completed and feel the happiness knowing that it has been manifested correctly without any flaws or errors.

Also visualize a color that represents your desire filling every part of your body. Do this for several minutes. While you do this, your brain sends off electromagnetic charges of what it is that you desire. Your blood picks up this electromagnetic energy and distributes it throughout your body.

Since all of your body has been charged with your desire, you may wish to use bodily items (such as blood, hair, urine, ejaculate, toe and finger nails, etc.) that you so desire to literally infuse the housing object with your desire. (Remember the suggestion for a cavity in the housing? This is where that would come into play) By doing this, the object is charged with your desire, which allows it to attract the correct type of entity energy to complete and manifest your desires (likes attracting likes).

Jews of biblical time held blood as a very sacred item, and understood that blood contained the fiery magickal life force of creation. They would sprinkle the blood of sacrificed animals on things that they wished to purify. Alchemists and other occultists believe that during the initial creation the entity should be fed blood of the creator. This blood was thought to carry the life force to the entity being created.

It has also been thought that by correctly manipulating sexual energy and joining semen and menstrual blood together powerful magickal results can be produced and an entity can be given life.

Rabbi Judah Loew of Prague has been noted in many texts to have fashioned a clay form into the shape of a human. Through powers given to him by God he was able to breathe life into the clay figure. This clay creature was known as a golem. When Rabbi Loew created this golem he incorporated the four elements: Earth (through the use of clay for the body), Fire (it has been noted that Rabbi baptized the golem by spilling blood unto the body of the golem), Water (it is believed that Rabbi Loew ejaculated into a cavity present in the clay form), and Air (it is believed that Rabbi Loew breathed into the nostrils of the golem). Rabbi Loew noted that because of the magickal origins of his golem, it could not be injured by the four elements.

To animate the housing object, you must constantly try to find ways to build unions with it. Some occultists suggest mixing ashes (Air and Fire), soil (Earth), water (well you get the idea) to represent the four elements along with your personal elements of blood (internal Fire), urine (Water), hair and/or nails (Earth), and breath (Air). This mixture is to be added into the entity's housing object.

Now state the name of the entity. For example: "I name you (entity's name), and from this day until (time of dissolution) you shall be known by this name." You may want to vibrate the name of the entity while visualizing the essence of the entity, as it possesses the housing object.

Breath is considered powerful and can have a large role in charging an object with the entity. This breath can be in the form of blowing, chanting, speaking, singing, etc. By using breath in the charging of the object, you play a role of a god by "breathing life" into the object. This act can have a significant psychological effect, and can aid in the relationship bonding between the entity and yourself.

When your blood reaches your lungs, while you are charging yourself with the essence of the entity, your breath becomes charged with your desires. When you feel that your body and breath have been charged with as much energy as they can take, slowly release your breath onto the housing object that you wish to charge. At the same time visualize the color that represents your desire flowing from yourself into the entity's housing object (or into the astral plane if no housing object is being used for this entity) filling every bit of it with that color.

Then say, "It is through my will that I now call you into being. You are given life to perform [entity's task(s)] to the benefit of all that may be involved harming none along your way." (This last section "to the benefit...harming none along your way," would obviously be reworded if the entity were to cause havoc for a person or group of people. Make sure you reword it to benefit and not harm you and any others that you do not wish to be harmed.)

Pick up the programming symbol and say, "With this symbol I am able to contact you with ease and at any time that I so desire, but (entity's name) when this symbol is no more, so shall your life and purpose be no more, for this is my will and so it is done. "

Release the entity and instruct it to go forth and manifest your desires by saying, "Go in peace (entity's name) and begin your task(s), remembering to appear quickly to me when called upon. If you have not completed your task by (time of dissolution), then disperse and cease to exist nonetheless. Be on your way!"

The former was just one way to charge the entity and/or programming symbol. Experiment with a variety of materials to create a programming symbol. Use ink pens, markers, or crayons to draw it, or perhaps use a wood burner to burn it into the housing. Many magi, as suggested earlier, use blood (if you are female, and if appropriate, you may want to take advantage of your menstrual blood as well). Draw it on parchment, wood, metal, cardboard, or even your body.

Do not limit yourself in the materials you use. Get creative with your activation; draw a symbol on your body with soap crayons and then take a bath. As the soap dissolves into the water off your body, the water receives that programming and activates the entity. Draw it on paper and feed it to a fire. Maybe draw it in the dirt and let the rain wash it away. These three examples make use of the elements (earth, air, fire, water). Or, you can make cookies in the form of the programming symbol or frost a cake with your symbol on it and eat it. If you practice sex magick, use body paints to draw the symbol. The symbol will be charged with the sexual energies and the entity activated when the symbol is either sweated off, when you achieve orgasm, or whatever you decide.

When charging an object, it is best to do so with great respect and care for the entity, and while in the proper mindset. The entity should be treated as you would treat yourself, as the entity will treat you in the same manner as it is treated. It is foolish to make enemies needlessly, this is just as true when working with entities as it is when working with human beings. The attention shown during the creation process must be sincere.

## Closing

This is where you would make a statement noting the magickal working is over and the entity has been "born" and is working on your desire. Typically most occultists do some form of reversal of the balancing (banishing) rite performed at the beginning of the magickal working. The Closing by Watchtower, or something similar, could be performed at this time.

Think of all the different ways you can incorporate all of the senses into your work so that it encompasses your entire self. Craft your entity carefully and thoughtfully. What you put into something is what you get out of it. Take your time with the creation, and in doing so you will insure a quality entity with quality tasks that are accomplished as you see fit.

# CONTACTING YOUR ENTITY

Once the entity has possessed the housing object, you are able to work with the entity in the manner desired. The manner in which you contact your entity can take many forms, be it invocation, evocation (summoning), petitions, prayers, etc. These acts confirm and strengthen the union between the entity and you. Ultimately, the method used to call upon your entity is up to you.

One of the most common forms of working with entities is through the magickal technique known as evocation. Evocation is calling something forth to work with it, or to have it work for you. Once the basics of evocation are mastered, you can accomplish great things with relative ease.

There are some people and books that warn against "conjuring" and the evocation of spirits. Most of these warnings are products of superstition, fear of the unknown, and ignorance. Usually these same people warn against using talking boards, holding séances, looking in a mirror over your shoulder in the dark, etc. for fear of contacting things from the "other side." These types of fears tend to be manifestations of the people's own fear of death and dying and what may be waiting for them on the "other side." Many people are quick to believe stories of a séance gone wrong, or a talking board bursting into flames, because they hold these same ignorant fears of death and the life hereafter. Other warnings only serve to keep people new to the subject of magick from veering off into areas of advanced magick before they have mastered the basics. Some of these warnings are very dire and even threaten life if ever used. It is our opinion, however, that if you have read this far into this book, you either do not believe the superstitious and ignorant warnings, you have "advanced" far enough to learn what is in this book, you are a very curious person, you don't give a damn about what other people think, or all of the above—if so, you have gained our respect.

When you need help from your entity, or wish to work with it, the following is a very easy and effective way to evoke your entity. When you have the thing that you need the entity's help with in front of you, or have an image of it in your mind, call the entity to you using mental imagery. Visualize your entity entering the thing that you need help with. See your entity grow through subject like air filling a child's balloon. Picture the entity expanding throughout the subject until its energy surrounds the subject. Continue to hold this visualization until you have received the feeling that all that can be done has been done. Then send a caring and respectful thought to the entity thanking it for its work. Then visualize the entity returning to its place of resting.

For example, you may be stuck in a traffic jam. You would visualize the entire traffic jam in your mind. Then you would visualize your "traffic jam entity" going into the core of the traffic jam. You would then visualize the entity growing until it has encompassed the entire traffic problem. You would visualize the entity doing whatever work may be necessary to return the traffic to a normal state and moving without restriction. After you feel that all that can be done has been done, mentally thank your entity and let it know that it may return to what every it was doing prior to you calling upon it.

Amanda uses either the programming symbol or a scent that calls the entity to her. David typically uses the programming symbol or visualizes the entity manifesting before him. Taylor uses the paintings he's made to represent the entity in question.

Some use what is known as a powerword. A powerword is a word that uses the vibrations of sound to energize and manipulate what occurs around you. Such a word can also be used to create or call entities once they are created. The word, when uttered, should call to mind the emotion and the visualization of the entity. Be sure that your visualization is as detailed as possible as you are only relying on your own voice to trigger the visualization of the entity. The entity and the word should be as one and when you say the word, you should feel power arise that calls forth the entity to do what you wish it to do. Vocalize the word, which is to say you mentally say the word to yourself, over and over again, until you build the energy up and the word pours forth from your mouth, thus evoking the enity.

There are many other ways to evoke and work with your entity. A great number of books on the subject of evocation have been written. Some of them include other simple ways to evoke things, and most of them include the same steps that were suggested earlier in this book, in the section explaining how you can give life to your entity. (Instead of giving life to the entity, however, you would evoke the entity and work with it.) We do not wish to replicate the work of others, so if you are interested in learning more about this subject, we suggest that you seek out books on the topic of evocation and talk with people that have a firm grasp on the subject.

To gain rapport with the entity, you could do daily meditations with your entity. To do this, sit in a comfortable area where you are able to view the entity's housing object, programming symbol, or both. Gaze at either of the entity objects while allowing your focus to blur a little. Relax as much as you can, and try to remove any miscellaneous thoughts that you may have at the time. You may begin to receive mental pictures or images. These images are the way that your entity communicates with your subconscious.

During these times, project respect and caring images to your entity. When you are done, remember to thank your entity for the opportunity of working with it.

There may be times where you find yourself in a situation where you specifically need to do something involving your entity's realm of influence. You may wish to invoke (calling the entity inside of you—this is the opposite of evocation) your entity to aid you in your actions. Then, after invoking your entity, it acts through you and all of your actions, from that point onwards, should be those of the entity, until you choose to end the invocation.

To make personal invocation easier between your entity and yourself, you should take every opportunity to study and understand the realm of influence of the entity. This way you will form a stronger bond with your entity, and through the magickal formulation of "likes attract likes," your workings with the entity will become easier and more productive, and you will notice a higher success rate of your magickal working with your entity.

The more sincere the contact is, the quicker you may begin to see the entity's housing object animate. After some time, it will become progressively easier to see the object come to action with little effort. With even more work, however, you may even begin to see your entity (in some form or fashion) away from the object in which it resides. This usually only happens when you have developed great psychic abilities.

You may even begin to hear sounds from your entity. When the entity reaches a higher state of life, you may even begin to feel the touch of the entity. Most of the time, your entity's touch will feel like spider webs. Then it may begin to feel like regular physical contact with a solid object. People have noted that the times between being awake and sleeping are the most common times of seeing, hearing, or feeling their entities.

# Preparation Guide

By now you have developed a solid background on the creation of entities. By mixing and matching magickal practices from your own magickal system, you will soon progress to working with advanced entity creation aspects. By using the worksheet that follows, and referring to the information in this book, you have everything you need to create any entity that you desire, from the simplest to the most complex.

**Basic Outline Of Entity Creation:**

- Define your goals
- Understand the purpose of your entity
- Create a name for your entity
- Define its appearance
- Choose its housing object
- Determine its source of energy
- Define its magickal abilities
- Determine the life span for your entity
- Decide the method(s) of dissolution, if appropriate
- Create your entity's programming symbol
- Give life to your entity
- Allow the entity to perform its task
- Perform the dissolution of your entity if appropriate

Of course some cases will require that these actions be performed in a slightly different arrangement. Other cases will require only a handful of these steps. It is up to you to decide what will be the most appropriate for your situation.

Use your instincts and intuition whenever you take on the task of creating magickal entities. If there is ever a time that some instruction or suggestion just doesn't sit right with you, go with what your heart says to do, because more often than not, it will be what is right for you.

If you feel that you are not sure of something, or that you may need to read a section again, go back and read that section again. Take your time so that you can understand the theories and ideas that are presented. There is no rush for you to get through this material as quickly as possible. The more thoroughly that you understand this material and the ideas presented in this book, the more rapidly your magickal workings will manifest your desires.

The worksheet in the next section is provided so that you may have a model to use when trying to organize your thoughts. It is basically self explanatory and relatively uncomplicated. In Appendix A you will find an example of how Amanda used the worksheet to formulate an inspiration entity. You do not have to use the worksheet provided, but you may find it helpful to use some form of record-keeping system. That way you do not have to rely on your memory when trying to create your entity.

It is important to record your experiences. You will then have a record that shows you where you succeeded or failed when you created an entity and set it to its task. By recording your experiences, you can draw on those experiences to show other people what you have accomplished as well as keeping yourself up-to-date on whatever you are working on.

When recording your experiences, ask yourself the following questions. What variables of reality did I factor into the creation and usage of the entity? What did I not factor in and how can I do so next time? What method of creation did I feel was most effective for the usage of entities (e.g., painting, powerwords, sculpting, etc.)? What was the need I made the entity for and did the entity fulfill that need? How can I improve on my entity? There are many more questions you can ask yourself, but these will give you a starting point.

Be thorough in recording your workings with the entity. By doing this, it will help make clear what it is you've done. It will also help you when you are looking back on past workings so that you can more easily draw upon them for workings in the future.

**Entity Creation Worksheet**

Date: ___/___/___

Goals and Desires: _____

_____

_____

Desired Results: _____

_____

Statement of Intent: _____

Abbreviated (Distilled) Statement of Intent: _____

General Realm of Influence: _____

Specific Realm of Influence: _____

Name:

Appearance:

Housing:

Energy Source/Feeding:

Magickal Abilities:

Life Span:

Method of Dissolution:

Colors:

Fragrance:

Moon Phase:

[  ] New Moon      [  ] Waxing Moon      [  ] Full Moon      [  ] Waning Moon

Day of Week:

[  ] Monday      [  ] Tuesday      [  ] Wednesday      [  ] Thursday

[  ] Friday      [  ] Saturday      [  ] Sunday

Hour (Planetary or otherwise):

Elements:

Day and Time of Creation:

Tools and Equipment Needed:

Programming Symbol:

Notes:

Results:

Questions:

# Entity Adaptations

After you have mastered the basics of entity creation, you may wish to experiment with adaptations to further your magickal workings. Entity adaptations help provide you with more versatility and flexibility in your workings. Some people like to think of entity adaptations as "advanced entity creation." Whatever kind of fancy title that you would like to place on it, entity adaptations can prove very beneficial to the success of your magickal workings.

There are entities that are known as general purpose, or general service, entities. These entities are fashioned with only a general realm of influence. The advantage of creating a general service entity is to have an entity "on call" that is able to work on any type of issue within a set field, say for example health. Every time you may have a health issue, you could call upon your health entity to help you out—sort of like a general practitioner doctor. The more that you use your health entity, the more power it receives. That power increases its ability to help you. Another example could be an entity of transportation. You could call upon this type of entity to help you get the best parking places in an emergency, help ease up traffic jams, have the bus run on time, help to fix a problem with your bike, etc. If you want to focus the entity to a specific task, your general entity can become specialized so that for instance the health entity becomes a dentist entity.

Some people have found that by telling other people about their entity, and showing how to use it when they need it, their entities have grown very powerful and have improved their magickal abilities. Something that helps boost the power of your general service entity is to attribute to the entity any success that falls in its general realm of influence, even if the entity was not called on. This will serve to strengthen your belief in its power, which will lead to more successes in its workings.

There are entities that you can create that either replicate themselves, produce "slave" entities, or both if certain conditions are met or not met. These type of entities are viral entities, as Phil Hine refers to them in his book *Condensed Chaos*. In their most simplistic of forms, these entities replicate in the manner of viruses to accomplish a set goal. If designed to do so, your entity could continue to replicate itself until its task has been completed. This type of entity works great in destroying illnesses and disease.

Have you ever wished that you had just a bit more magickal energy during a working? Have you ever wished that you could tap into an energy reserve to help out with a healing? Well now you can, if you create an Energy Store-House Entity (ESHE). An ESHE's sole purpose is to collect, store, and distribute energy on demand. This type of entity is created to store energy that is given to it at times when you feel full of energy or power, but have nothing to do with it. It then collects this energy and stores it, waiting for you to call upon it to deliver the energy back you. Even if you feed negative energy to it after you have been in an argument, your ESHE could have been instructed, during creation, to remove all emotion from the energy and to store only the pure, raw energy for your use.

You can adapt an ESHE to collect neutral forms of energy, like the light from a lamp being left on when it is not needed, to add to your energy to increase the power available to you. If you do this, it may be a good idea to be very specific as to what type of energy it collects, and how it collects it. There have been some ill prepared magi that have accidentally created energy "vampires" that would collect any type of energy they can, even from people.

You can also use this sort of entity to send energy to other people. If, for example, a friend of yours was just in an accident, you cannot be there for them and you do not have the time or ability to do a full magickal ritual for them, you could, however, send your ESHE to deliver energy to them—it sure "one ups" the typical "I'll light a candle for you" cliché spewed by so many.

An alternative energy entity was touched on earlier in the book, but it deserves to be expanded upon. Creating and maintaining an entity can be hard work at times, depending on how you set things up. Some entities require large amounts of energy, energy that you may not be able or have the time to give. In these instances, you may want to look into using alternative forms of energy management. An example of this type of entity could be an entity used by a salesperson. This person could create an entity that would stimulate sales. For whatever reason, our salesperson does not have the time to feed the entity, so the salesperson instructs the entity to feed off of the energy of any and every sale ever made in every location in the city in which the salesperson lived. This way, the salesperson has supplied the entity with a reliable supply of energy. Also, by feeding the entity "sales" energy, it will improve the entity's working because it directly relates to the entity's task—stimulate more sales for the salesperson. If you think about it long enough, you can probably come up with hundreds of ideas of alternatively feeding your entity. Remember to make it as closely related to the entity's task as possible for a better chance success.

If you have a desire to work with a commonly known spirit, deity, or entity, you can create a personal entity to act as a link with it by developing a name, image, and symbol based on the characteristics of the inspirational subject. You can even decide upon a specific realm of influence based on the general realm of influence of the original spirit or deity. By doing this, you are personalizing a link with the original subject through the creation of a personal entity. From that point on, you can call upon the spirit or deity through the name and symbol that you have designated to elicit a direct response from the desired entity. It is important to remember that you are working with an entity that serves as a link to the spirit or deity and not the spirit or deity itself. After continuous workings, you can, if you so desire, have the entity you created evolve away from the original spirit or deity to become its own independent entity. Then when you work with your entity, you will be working with your entity alone, though it will have gained knowledge and experience through the old link with the spirit or deity.

The same idea can be used to make an entity based on the aspects of a living or dead person. By taking the person's name and personal attributes, a very powerful and viable entity can be formed. This new entity will be linked to both the person and to you, in a similar fashion to an entity providing a link to a deity or spirit. This type of entity, when linked to a living person, can have great and powerful affects upon them. With such a link, an entity can be very useful for works of healing and protection directed at the person to whom it is linked. Of course, you can also use this sort of entity to inflict many dire things upon a person, should you so desire.

# Epilogue

The material presented in this book will help you along your path of magickal progression. This information provides you with the mechanics of successful entity creation, along with the tools to develop your own system of entity creation. What you create depends entirely on how much effort that you would like to put forth.

Entity creation isn't for everybody. People wishing to work with spirits may not feel comfortable with creating their own entities or spirits. However, if you are interested in taking your magick to the next level, then magickal entity creation may be just the thing for you. Don't take our word for it; try it out for yourself.

While it is good to take the things you do seriously, it is important to remember that entity creation is fun. The fear of making mistakes should not restrict you to being a rigid drone. We've made our share of mistakes and we are still here. As long as you learn from any mistakes that may occur, there is no reason why you should view magickal entity creation, or any magickal working, for that matter, as anything other than a fun and educational experience.

We hope that this book has inspired you to take the theories of magickal entity creation and incorporate them into your magickal system. If not, we at least hope that you will take this information and view your magick in a different manner.

If you have enjoyed this book and have an Internet connection, we would greatly appreciate it if you let other people know about it by leaving a favorable review at Amazon.com and barnesandnoble.com. Even if you don't have an internet connection, we would appreciate any efforts made in letting other people know about this book. (A great way would be to ask your local library, local bookseller, or both, if they carry this book. If they say they don't, politely request that they do.)

If you aren't satisfied with this book, neither are we. Let us know how we can improve it. You may send us mail in care of the publisher (the address is listed at the front of this book), or you can send us an email (the addresses are listed below).

May all of your magickal workings be strong and full of life. May all of your magickal entity creations bring you much happiness.

You may contact us at the following email addresses:

David can be reached at:
dcunningham@EgregorePublishing.com

Taylor can be reached at:
tellwood@EgregorePublishing.com

Amanda can be reached at:
awagener@EgregorePublishing.com

Chat with others online about magickal entities at:

http://groups.yahoo.com/group/Geist-Project

# APPENDIX A

## Inspiration Entity Worksheet
*by Amanda R. Wagener*

**Date:** 09/06/2002

**Goals and Desires:** To provide the user with inspiration and to remove hindrances that would get in the way of the user completing his or her work.

> *Notes:* The reason why this entity was created was to help my creativity and to inspire me in my work. Since I have been writing more, I have found that I would lose my inspiration after a while, and could not quite get motivated to continue. This came out much of the time while I was helping to write this book as well as while working on another book I am currently writing, Sigils and Other Magickal Symbols. I needed to be inspired about the topic of my writing. I wanted new ideas to come forth, which I knew were trapped in my mind, somewhere, but there seemed to be blockages. Originally, I had created a Sigil to address this, but then later found that an entity would be more appropriate to my needs.

**Desired Results:** Inspiration provided and/or hindrances removed.

> *Notes:* My desire for inspiration to be provided was only one part of my desired results as I have come to understand that sometimes by simply removing a hindrance, inspiration will come. The results I wanted are clearly stated; inspiration provided to me (or the user of this entity) and/or hindrances removed (if necessary for inspiration to come).

**Statement of Intent:** Names of Muses (Part 1), Words "Muse" and "Inspiration" (Part 2), "Remove Hindrances" (Part 3)

> *Notes:* I chose to be a bit unorthodox in my statement of intent. Since this was an inspiration entity, my first thoughts were of the Greek Muses. Muses inspire and since there were so many that covered a vast area of arts, I felt their energy was appropriate to put into this entity. I had decided to use all 15 Muses and not just the 9 most people are aware of today. I wanted to have the greatest amount of help available. The muses were only part one of my statement. Part two included the words "muse" and "inspiration" melded together to further infuse the entity with my desire. Finally, part three incorporated the part of removing hindrances. Since this entity helped with creativity, I wished to be as creative as possible with the construction of the entity

to put that creative energy into it. I was inspired to create this entity after creating my original inspiration sigil, so it was only suiting to incorporate such within my inspiration entity.

## Abbreviated (Distilled) Statement of Intent:

PART 1 (Greek Muses)

Listed names of all Greek Muses.
Melete, Mneme, Aoide.
Nete, Mese, Hypate.
Caliope, Clio, Euterpe, Thalia, Melpomene, Terpsichore, Erato, Polymnia, Urania.

> *Notes:* I chose the muses because they are associated with inspiring those interested in the arts and sciences. I used all 15 muses because I need as much help as I can. At first, three muses were worshipped on Mount Helicon in Boeotia: Melete ("meditation"), Mneme ("memory"), and Aoede ("song"). Another three were worshipped at Delphi and their names represented the names of the strings of a lyre: Nete, Mese, and Hypate. The Greeks finally established the nine muses, daughters of Zeus (king of the gods) and Mnemosyne ("memory", Caliope, Clio, Euterpe, Thalia, Melpomene, Terpsichore, Erato, Polymnia, Urania, who were born at Pieria at the foot of Mount Olympus.

Deleted all duplicated letters.

MELETE ~~MNEME~~ AOIDE ~~NETE MESE~~ HYPATE ~~CALIOPE~~
~~CLIO~~ EUTERPE ~~THALIA MELPOMENE TERPSICHORE~~
~~ERATO POLYMNIA URANIA~~
M E L T N A O I D S H Y P C U R

> *Notes:* Per "traditional" distillation methods,
> I deleted all duplicate letters to slim down the
> amount of letters.

Then deleted any letters that did not have Greek alphabet
equivalent.

M E L T N A O I D S ~~H Y~~ P C U R
M E L T N A O I D S P U R

> *Notes:* I decided to keep with the Greek theme
> and delete any letters that didn't have Greek
> alphabet equivalents. This was to help thin
> the list of letters.

Then converted letters to numbers.

| M | E | L | T | N | A | O | I | D | S | P | U | R |
|---|---|---|---|---|---|---|---|---|---|---|---|---|
| 4 | 5 | 3 | 2 | 5 | 1 | 6 | 9 | 4 | 1 | 7 | 3 | 9 |

Then deleted repeating numbers.

4 5 3 2 5 1 6 9 4 ~~1~~ 7 ~~3 9~~
4 5 3 2 1 6 9 4 7

> *Notes:* Using the Pythagorean system, I
> converted letters to numbers so I could delete
> the duplicate numbers since there were still
> too many to work with.

| 1 | 2 | 3 | 4 | 5 | 6 | 7 | 8 | 9 |
|---|---|---|---|---|---|---|---|---|
| A | B | C | D | E | F | G | H | I |
| J | K | L | M | N | O | P | Q | R |
| S | T | U | V | W | X | Y | Z |   |

Converted back into letters.

| 4 | 5 | 3 | 2 | 1 | 6 | 9 | 7 |
|---|---|---|---|---|---|---|---|
| M | E | L | T | A | O | I | P |

Then transliterated into Greek letters.

> *Notes:* The letters did not look appealing as is, so I decided to stay with the Greek theme and convert the letters into Greek letters to be used as Part 1 of the programming symbol.

PART 2 (Inspiration & Muse)

The word Inspiration is distilled by deleting duplicate letters.

I N S P I R A T I O N

I N S P R A T O

Further distillation by deleting every other letter.

I N S P R A T O

I S R T

Insert MUSE into distilled Inspiration.

| I |   | S |   | R |   | T |   |
|---|---|---|---|---|---|---|---|
|   | M |   | U |   | S |   | E |
| **I** | **M** | **S** | **U** | **R** | **S** | **T** | **E** |

> *Notes:* Again, per "traditional" distillation methods, I deleted all duplicate letters to slim

down the amount of letters. Since there were still too many, I decided on a whim to delete every other letter. This resulted in four letters being left, which was exactly what I needed since I wanted to evenly meld "inspiration" and "muse."

Convert letters to numbers.

| I | M | S | U | R | S | T | E |
|---|---|---|---|---|---|---|---|
| 9 | 4 | 1 | 3 | 9 | 1 | 2 | 5 |

Notes: These numbers will be used to construct Part 2A of the programming symbol using a magick square.

| Magick Square | | |
|:---:|:---:|:---:|
| 4 | 9 | 2 |
| 3 | 5 | 7 |
| 8 | 1 | 6 |

Added numbers, then distilled until single digit number.
9+4+1+3+9+1+2+5=34, 3+4=7

*Notes:* This number will be used to construct Part 2B of the programming symbol.

PART 3 (Remove Hindrances)

Deleted all duplicated letters.

REMOVE HINDRANCES

R E M O V H I N D A C S

Then converted letters to numbers.

| R | E | M | O | V | H | I | N | D | A | C | S |
|---|---|---|---|---|---|---|---|---|---|---|---|
| 9 | 5 | 4 | 6 | 4 | 8 | 9 | 5 | 4 | 1 | 3 | 1 |

Then deleted repeating numbers.

9 5 4 6 4 8 9 5 4 1 3 1

9 5 4 6 8 1 3

*Notes:* Per "traditional" distillation methods, I deleted all duplicate letters to slim down the amount of letters, then converted to numbers because there were too many letters, and deleted duplicate numbers.

Added numbers and distilled to single digit number.

9+5+4+6+8+1+3=36, 3+6=9

*Notes:* This number will be used to construct Part 3 of the programming symbol.

**General Realm of Influence:** Inspiration

**Specific Realm of Influence:** Excellent provider of inspiration and hindrance removal.

**Name:** Emer Ipsni

*Notes:* I chose the name by writing, "inspire me" backwards out of convenience.

**Appearance:**

| Letter | Body Part | Number | Sex | Looks |
|--------|-----------|--------|-----|-------|
| E | Head | 5 | M | writer |
| M | Neck | 4 | F | sculptor |
| E | Shoulders | 5 | M | writer |
| R | Chest/ Arms | 9 | M | musician |
| I | Stomach | 9 | M | artist |
| P | Buttocks | 7 | M | editor |
| S | Thighs | 1 | M | writer |
| N | Shins | 5 | M | writer |
| I | Feet | 9 | M | journalist |

**Sex:** Male

*Notes:* I decided on the appearance by using the technique mentioned in this book. Sex was determined by going off the majority of the nature of the numbers, which was overwhelmingly masculine. I found this interesting since all of the muses are female. I felt this makes the entity very balanced.

**Housing:** A bottle bearing the programming symbol that is holding the scent of the entity.

*Notes:* I chose a bottle to hold a scent because I liked the idea of activating the entity by the sense of smell. I had envisioned this bottle to be a pendant to be hung around the neck so that the entity can be called upon at any time.

**Energy Source/Feeding:** Hybrid of personal energy, devotional plates of water, milk, or honey, and hindrances.

> *Notes:* I chose the hybrid model because I did not want the entity to rely solely on me for energy. Since part of the actions of the entity is to remove hindrances, I felt that it would be good for the entity to feed off those hindrances. Also, the more the entity feeds off a particular hindrance, the easier time it will have removing the hindrance in the future. Hindrances will be removed more quickly and completely. Personal energy and devotional plates is energy the entity would be getting from me directly. Personal energy is like a special treat for the entity and comes with an energy boost. The reason why there are specifics with the devotional plates is because sacrifices to the Muses consisted of liberations of water, milk, and honey.

**Magickal Abilities:** Remove hindrances (mainly by feeding off them) and inspiring user in whatever project or working they need inspiration.

**Life Span:** When the original creator's life ceases, so shall the entity's life, unless the original creator intentionally destroys the housing.

> *Notes:* Since I anticipate using this entity for a long time, it seemed appropriate to have it

last as long as I did, or until I felt I no longer
needed it.

**Method of Dissolution:** By intentionally destroying the
entity's housing.

**Colors:** Yellow

> *Notes:* Yellow is a colour of the arts,
> expression, and of course, inspiration.
> Yellow is also the colour that symbolizes Air
> and the East.

**Fragrance:** Lemon

> *Notes:* The smell of lemon is fresh and tends
> to wake up the mind, so it is appropriate
> to the purpose of this entity. Lemons are
> yellow, so it aligns with some of the other
> correspondences.

**Moon Phase:** Waxing Moon during creation.

> *Notes:* I chose this because the waxing cycle
> is used to begin new projects. First Quarter
> is usually associated with the East and the
> Element Air.

**Day of Week:** Friday

> *Notes:* It just so happened that the First
> Quarter Moon happened on a Friday. I
> wanted the moon to be half lit showing the
> balance between light and dark, feminine
> and masculine, and all other dual forces.

**Hour (Planetary or otherwise):** Dawn

> *Notes:* The birth of a new day. I feel an appropriate time to give life to an entity of this type.

**Elements:** Air

> *Notes:* Air is the element of the East, which is the direction of mental attributes. The scent will be released into the Air.

**Day and Time of Creation:** Friday, September 13, 2002 at Dawn

> *Notes:* It was a First Quarter Moon.

**Programming Symbol:**

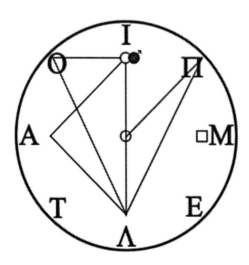

*Notes:* I placed the beginning letter of Part 1 in the East of the programming symbol as East represents the element Air and is the direction of beginnings, vision, creativity, intellectual growth, the arts, and most of all, inspiration. I continued around clockwise with each letter, one in each direction (E, SE, S, SW, W, NW, N, NE). I was also happy that there were eight letters, as I like to work in the directions. This to me represented the cycle of creativity—the birth of the idea, growth, life, and eventually transformation.

Using Part 2A information, drew a circle at start number 9, and then connected to each number with a line, ending with a circle at number 5. Using Part 2B information, I then placed a square at the number 7.

Using Part 3 information, I was going to place a darkened circle at the number 9, but there was already a circle there, so I placed one next to it, but somewhat layered on top of it.

I wanted to place a symbol of the sex of the entity within the programming symbol. So I took the name numbers (thus incorporating the name as well) and added the numbers and distilling to a single digit number    (5+4+5+9+9+7+1+5+9=54, 5+4=9). It was interesting that the total was nine as the number nine is a masculine number, which was also the sex of the entity. I placed a male symbol at the number 9 on top of the darkened circle.

The number nine kept coming up when creating this entity. Nine means preparation of new ground for development, mental growth, success, achievement, and creative expression. This, although unintentional, was a good thing in regards to the entity.

**Tools and Equipment Needed:**    Bottle, necklace, yellow paint to paint programming symbol on bottle, lemon essential oil

# Appendix B

## Esacniw
*by David Michael Cunningham*

On Oct. 26, of 2001, I had to go to court for something that happened back in 1996. Because of the circumstances, I was unable to take care of the issue back then. But in 2001, I had to take care of it.

As the date drew near, I started to become concerned as to the outcome. I was guilty and was especially concerned because of where the incident occurred, as the judge in that area likes make examples of people by punishing them to the fullest extent possible.

Anyway I was looking at a possible six months in jail and a $1,000 fine, not including court costs. I knew that I would not get the full six months, but I didn't know how many days I would get. I also knew I would not get charged the full amount of the fine either, but I didn't know how much that I would get hit with.

OK, now you know the mentality that I held. As the date was drawing near, I wondered if the judge would try to punish me in a harsh way. I decided to create an entity to help me out.

My desire was to not go to jail and not to pay any fines. So I decided that my entity should be a very large influential lawyer. This lawyer knows all of the legal loopholes and knows how to bend the law if there is no loophole that will help win the case. This lawyer carries around a brief case that contains a laptop computer that he can use to connect with any legal database in the world.

This lawyer entity would serve to provide legal council to my lawyer. The entity also bends the will of any judge to provide a favorable outcome for the person that the entity is servicing.

I decided to infuse the powers of Saturn (to break down barriers and bring swift endings to things), Jupiter (for luck, intellectual influence, and divine majesty), Mercury (for wisdom, inspiration, and intellectual greatness), Mars (for the ability to withstand courtroom battles, the ability to do battle and win any time it is needed, The skill to succeed in any court case), and the Moon (for over all protection, and to add to the power of my magick).

I took the astrological signs of these planets and constructed a programming symbol with them. I took my desire, "serve no time, pay no fines," and reduced it down to the numbers 8 and 2. Normally I would reduce them down further, to 1, but the numbers 8 and 2 had some qualities that I knew the entity would need to bring forth my desires. So I added the number 8 and the number 2 to the programming symbol. The programming symbol was made with the color purple for luck and to bring a strong influence from Jupiter.

I charged the programming symbol and created the entity through the use of sex magick. I decided that it would be good to use my wife for the ritual because she has a strong desire for me to not serve any time and to pay no fines.

I created the ritual incense with sandalwood, white sage, and wormwood. I used this incense to charge the room with the magickal intent and I balanced my wife's energy with the smoke of the ritual incense.

We then consumed a very large glass of blood red wine. The wine's color was used to symbolize the blood and life energy of the entity that we were going to "give birth to." The wine's other use was to put us into an altered state quickly, as we had to start and end this ritual during the 23rd hour of Saturday (the hour of Jupiter and the day of Saturn).

I summoned forth the ancient powers that the entity was to be born with. We aligned our energies with the powers present (that was kind of odd feeling, as I felt that at this point I was able to do anything that I had ever wanted—a real awesome feeling). I then presented my wife with a copy of the programming symbol for her to focus on during the sexual part of the ritual. I took my copy of the programming symbol and placed it next to her. She was on her back and I climbed on top of her in the missionary position and inserted my penis into her vagina. While I was inserting and withdrawing, I was speaking out loud all of the "programming" that was to be the core DNA of the entity.

As I became close to ejaculate, I withdrew my penis and began to manually stimulate myself. I took my copy and placed it onto my wife's stomach and ejaculated onto the programming symbol. During the ejaculation, I ran a picture through my head, of me being dismissed from court not having to pay any fines and serving any time.

When done with the ejaculation, I took up the soaked programming symbol and burned it into the incense. We then opened a window (we were very lightheaded with all of the smoke) and placed the incense container on the windowsill to allow the smoke to give free reign to the entity Esacniw (Pronounced: "E sack new"—the backward spelling of "win case").

During the week before the court date, any time that I started to think about the case, I would chant in my head the name of Esacniw until my mind dropped the thought. While chanting I would force what ever my thought about the case was, to me being dismissed from court not having to pay any fines and not serve any time.

On the day of the court date, I slipped into the court-room after talking with my lawyer. I envisioned seeing Esacniw changing court papers around, looking into his brief case updating things, and prepping my lawyer.

Now, here is a strange thing, I noticed that almost every case before mine was "dismissed" and the people were only to pay court costs. The few people that didn't get off so lucky, only had to pay a small part of their fines, and were basically let off with a stinging hand slap.

It was at this point that I started to wonder, "What is going on?" This judge never does this. I started to think, "Watch this stuff stop just as soon as I get up there." As soon as that thought left, I started to chant in my head Esacniw's name and visualized me being dismissed without having to pay any fines and serving time.

I was up—it was time to see my work in action. My lawyer rambled some things very quickly to the judge. I was only able to pick out a few things. The judge then responded with, "twenty days incarceration and two hun-dred fifty dollar fine…" I was like, "What the…? This can't be happening!" Then the judge finished his statement with, "…suspended." I was astonished. He then rambled on about some other things that I couldn't make out. He then came to the other issue and waived that. He ordered that I only pay court costs. The entity had worked.

# Appendix C

## Cerontis
*by Taylor Ellwood*

I created this entity, Cerontis, with the specific purpose of finding opportunities for me to exploit to my advantage. Or in other words the entity makes me aware of possibilities I can use to improve myself, and to further my agenda in this world. The benefits of the entity are invaluable. Not only does it watch out for my potential interests, but also it makes me aware of those interests. I still need to act on the notifications I'm given. The entity doesn't make the possibility reality, only I do that. But by being made more aware of possibilities I lose out less than the average person who may miss opportunities for the simple fact that he or she didn't know what was going on around him or her.

I operate this entity on the principle that it's better that I take the action in making the possibility a reality. So, in essence I still play a key part in the process of making the possibility a reality. The entity is my bloodhound and finds the possibilities that I can use to my best advantage. To do otherwise is to put the power in its hand and give it the means to change my life. Now you might argue that by having it notify me of what could happen it is changing my life, but in truth it is only giving me information. I must choose whether or not to act on that information. Whatever choice I make becomes my responsibility, but still gives me the power to decide how my life shall be.

I created this entity on my birthday, using my personal energies to bind it to the painting I'd created for it. I have given the entity a life span of one year, which gives it lots of time to show me how useful it is to me. This type of entity is easy to create if you bear in mind that you need to be able to think in terms of probable realities, which is to say you need to think in more dimensions than the ones that you inhabit. You can make an entity like Cerontis when you can experience alternate realities at the same time that you experience this reality. Only with that kind of understanding of reality will you be able to affect reality and for that matter, get information on the various types of reality that could be.

To explain what I mean by alternate realities first consider that Cerontis is a Time/space Entity, in and of itself. This means that this entity primarily deals with the dimensions of time/space. So this entity has to be able to comprehend several things. First it must comprehend that time is not linear, but rather non-linear. Time is also a function of space. That is to say that without space time could not exist, because space gives it the means to occur. Third time/space is a frame of mind, a way of thinking. In order for us to deal with time/space and the possibilities it presents us, we must think of time in certain ways. Most people think of time as a linear progression. One moment occurs after the other. The problem with this frame of thinking is that these people are subject to time and accordingly live a very stressed out existence. They miss out on a lot of opportunities because they are very focused on making one moment happen right after another instead of considering that time can be non-linear and can accordingly present you with many different opportunities in one moment.

Cerontis works on the principle that time and space are non-linear, that in fact multiple realities can exist in one moment. I call these multiple realities "possibilities" and you can consider those possibilities to be opportunities. Although I tend to think non-linearly as far as time goes, I realize that it never hurts to have another set of eyes looking into possibilities for me. Cerontis scans the possibility field of time and picks out possibilities I may not be aware of it. It then informs me of the opportunity. It uses any number of mediums, such as people, events, information provided in books etc. to make me aware of the possibilities. Cerontis also scans the possibility field of time for favorable outcomes to those possibilities. When it presents the information to me, it presents it in a way that makes me very aware of the possible outcomes, so that I know the risk involved and can decide whether the possibility is worth pursuing.

This function that Cerontis serves allows me to focus on other matters at hand. Still for an entity to be effective like this you need to be able to think in non-linear terms. After all, it is how you understand time that determines how the entity will understand time. Some of the exercises recommended in this book will help in that matter. I also recommend thinking of time as not being linear, not being a moment that dictates what you do and when you do it, but rather non-linear which has you dictating what you do and when you do it. Don't live by anyone else's schedule. Instead learn to manage your time by being extremely aware of how time works and how to optimize what you do. Always know that you are choosing when to do something as opposed to having someone tell you when you will do it. If you have that mind frame you'll soon find that time does bend to your needs instead of you bending to it.

# Appendix D

## D'watcher
*by Amanda R. Wagener*

This entity was created in mid-1999 to toy with the inhabitants of a house in which I had previously lived. I was a bit vengeful at the time due to the circumstances of my moving out, and this entity provided the closure I needed. Would I do it again if I could? Probably not. I would most likely have used my energy to do other things.

I had drawn the entity's programming symbol on several thumbtacks and placed them throughout the house in places they would not be easily seen such as closets, under the carpet, and in cabinets. The entity was given life via a sex magick ritual with my partner. The fluids that were excreted by the both of us during this ritual were applied to a piece of paper which had the entity's programming symbol along with symbols appropriate to the tasks of the entity (e.g. broken pipes, water, broken windows, cracks, tripped breakers, termites, etc.).

I had nearly forgotten about the entity when I found out that a friend of mine had moved into the upper unit in which I used to live. He had told me about some mishaps he had when trying to fix some things in the unit. The first was the sink in the bathroom that he was trying to fix. He was attempting to fix the pipes underneath, but instead, the entire sink fell off the wall. The second issue was the kitchen sink, which he was trying to replace the pipes underneath, but the pipes kept falling apart every time he tried. Those were the two major things. I had not heard about any more issues with the unit from him, but he did move out in the early part of 2002.

Here was my worksheet that I used when I created the entity. These were notes for myself mainly, but also much of what I visualized during the ritual when I was giving birth to the entity.

**General Intent:** Slow Destruction of House and Frighten Inhabitants.

**Specific Intent:** To promote the slow destruction of the house located at [location] and to frighten its inhabitants by allowing them to see various ghosts, wraiths, and daemons.

**Symbols Appropriate To The Task:** Broken pipes, water, broken windows, cracks, tripped breakers, termites

**Life Span:** Five years, until destruction of structure, or until the house is sold. When any of these occur, the entity will follow [name of person] for three years and will continue with actions denoted by + (below).

**Name:** D'watcher (Destructive Watcher, [name of person] Watcher).

**Appearance:** Five feet tall, black skinned, female winged gargoyle with emerald green eyes, razor sharp claws. It has the ability to assume the appearance of daemons, ghosts, wraiths, etc.

**Programming Symbol:**

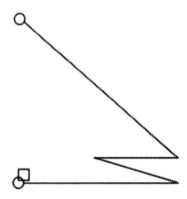

Placed in many locations throughout unit, carved in inside trim of doors, floorboards up in attic, underside of roof, shelves in closets, etc.

**Residence:** House (upper unit of the duplex)

**Feeding:** From the energies of the individuals that live at [location]

**Abilities:** Any efforts to improve house will increase entity's power (i.e. try to rent upper unit, plaster or paint walls, fix broken pipes, etc.). The more improvements, the more havoc caused, the more power the entity gains.

Once per day, entity will cause some kind of small destruction to the house. This may include breaking a window, causing a crack in the wall or ceiling, tripping a breaker, breaking a pipe, and encouraging termites to feast upon the house.

• Every time an individual finishes a cup of coffee, the entity assumes the appearance of a daemon, ghost, wraith, etc. and makes itself visible to the individuals for 3 minutes.

• Every time an individual talks about magickal arts of any type, the entity assumes a wraith-like appearance, retreats to a corner, and makes itself visible to the individuals for 2 minutes, then moves to another corner of the room for 2 minutes, then makes itself invisible.

• Every time an individual says the word "watcher," the entity will make an auditable growl for 10 seconds.

• Every attempt to "banish" or get rid of the entity will increase the entity's power.

# APPENDIX E

## The HP Entity
*by Taylor Ellwood*

One of the recent projects we have worked on is a Harry Potter entity. As many of you may know, some Christians were in a furor about Harry Potter. We first came up with the idea of the Harry Potter entity when we visited each other over Thanksgiving of 2001. I had read the Harry Potter series and had always noted with amusement how worked up some Christians got when talking about Harry Potter and his possible effect on children, i.e., getting them interested in witchcraft. We came up with the idea of creating an entity out of Harry Potter that would essentially take the negativity (the fear and hatred) of Christians and use that energy in an effort to stimulate an interest in the occult for the readers of Harry Potter. The entity acted like a viral entity in the sense that it would subvert the energy being used against it and convert that energy into an idea that would then "infect" readers of Harry Potter with an interest exploring further the occult. As can be seen, viral entities can work in a way that causes no harm, but instead promotes a cause. Now it should be noted the Harry Potter entity does not actively convert a person to the occult, but just stimulates an interest in finding out about it. Ultimately the person must decide whether or not he or she will look into the occult.

To create the entity we decided to look for some Harry Potter images on the Internet as well as some images of churches and a horde of people going into Hogwarts School of Witchcraft and Wizardry that Harry Potter attends in his adventures. We mixed these images together to form a collage that would represent our goals. We had Harry casting Magick, standing on a destroyed church and we also had him boiling the Pope in a cauldron. We had a horde of people entering into Hogwarts. Finally we made a message: "Couldn't We All Use A Little Magick?"

The next phase for the usage of this entity is to spread fliers with the collage on it to people, putting the fliers up around colleges and other places where the public will be exposed to the entity. A lot of people will rip down the fliers, but that suits the purpose of generating energy the entity can feed on so that it can increase an interest in the occult. Secondly if the fliers are left in place it will still get the attention of people and imprint an interest in the idea of exploring the occult. We then sent out the image online and explained the concept behind it to various magi that we knew. We asked them to charge it up and pass on the image to anyone else they knew.

The reports we received from the magi indicated success and in one case showed the danger of working with a viral entity. The mage charged the entity while listening to Christmas music on her portable CD player. Not only did the batteries temporarily stop working, but also the person felt ill. The entity sensed the Christian energy within the Christmas carols and drew from that energy to feed itself, and because the person was listening to that music, the entity fed off the person as well. The lesson in this case is to be careful in how you interact with an entity. They depend on energy just as we do and accordingly can feed off of a person.

# Appendix F

## Faerie of Lost Things
*by Amanda R. Wagener*

I have several statues and figurines of faeries in my house. I love faeries, so whenever I see a unique one, I have to bring her (or him) home.

I was once told the reason why things come up missing in your house is because the faeries probably "borrowed" it. See, faeries like things, especially shiny things, and they tend to be so entranced by it, they walk off with it. I have "lost" my keys and several CDs because of this.

One day, I had "misplaced" my keys. I looked everywhere. Finally, I got fed up and then something told me to ask my faeries—so, I did. I walked over to my faerie statues and asked if they would help me find my keys. I walked out to look for them again and within a few minutes, there they were, in plain sight! So of course I ran back to thank them—don't want to offend the faeries. I leave milk or honey for them sometimes or even bent pins.

My strong belief in the fae folk, as well as my belief that "they" could help, created a thought-form by simply believing it into being. The Faerie of Lost Things is a product of my own thoughts. However, it could also be an existing form that is merely conforming to an image I have created. It is absolutely necessary, in order to keep the thought-form alive, to believe in it. The mind can create any particular object desired; like children and their "living" dolls. But just as they were created to live, as soon as that belief is gone, the dolls will return to their previous state, that of just being a doll.

# APPENDIX G

## Divination Goddess
*by Taylor Ellwood*

An entity we, David, myself, and later Amanda, worked on together is our goddess-form of divination, Miss Cleo. Some of you may be familiar with the Miss Cleo commercials, the self-proclaimed Jamaican shaman, who advertises her divinatory services to people.

We thought about the idea that the character of Miss Cleo must be receiving the energies of the people who believe in her. If she is doing so, these energies will develop into an archetypal goddess form of Miss Cleo. This higher version of her is also comprised of the belief that people have in her skills as a tarot reader.

Bearing that in mind we began to think that it might be a novelty to actually use Miss Cleo as our goddess of divination, a being that would help us improve our divination abilities. David came up with some brilliant images we could use to focus our visualizations on Miss Cleo. We also watched her commercials and looked at any information on her to come up with attributes that we felt our version of Miss Cleo should have. Attributes are important as they can determine how helpful an entity can be. In the case of Miss Cleo we decided to focus on the following attributes: Knowledgeable, wise, compassionate, strong divination ability, ability to see possibilities, and empathy. We didn't focus in any way on her money making or anything that could be perceived as negative.

As far as we were concerned our version of Miss Cleo was a positive entity that could teach us about divination and that was all that mattered to us. When you model an entity after a person make sure you focus only on the attributes that will help you and when you come across attributes of that person that go against your version of the person ignore them, as they will only take away from the strength of your entity's work for you.

Think of it this way. For an entity such as our version of Miss Cleo to be effective for us we needed to have belief in the entity and specifically we needed to have belief in the attributes we assigned it. Belief is a very powerful tool, because belief is power. When I choose to believe in our version of Miss Cleo as a teacher entity of divination I am giving her power to affect me, but in doing so I am also giving myself an opportunity to learn more about divination through the teacher entity.

When David and I made our version of Miss Cleo we hinged a large part of the creation and feeding of the entity off of the attention that people gave her. Whether the attention was positive or negative we focused on the idea that our version of Miss Cleo could take that energy and make it into raw energy that would let her do an accurate reading and teach us divinatory skills. It has to this date proven to be very effective for divination and in fact for shaping reality through possibilities, which is all that divination really presents to a person.

David and I decided to invoke the Miss Cleo entity into ourselves and do a tarot reading. Mind you we did this on-line, as we lived in separate states at the time. Nonetheless we both found the readings to be very accurate and after the readings had occurred Miss Cleo took us both on a vision quest where we perceived each other even as we perceived her. When we later e-mailed each other, the details of our visions matched and so we had our first, but not last, successful working with the Miss Cleo entity.

Now it's important to note that we didn't so much create this entity as draw on the pop culture icon of Miss Cleo to fuel our own ideas of what Miss Cleo was to us. Nonetheless we did in a sense create our own Miss Cleo, a goddess of divination that would aid us in not only doing divinations, but also teaching us skills we could use in divination and in other forms of magick. We essentially tapped into the essence of the energy that Miss Cleo was getting from people who believed in her and in doing so we found what we needed.

Now we have worked with the Miss Cleo entity individually, but for this book we're going to focus on the work we did together with Miss Cleo. We have only done one other working with Miss Cleo together. Amanda joined us when we did this working. David supplied the images and we focused first on empowering the Miss Cleo entity, giving it the focus of what it is was we wanted to achieve with our working, namely becoming divinatory seers like herself. After we charged up the images of Miss Cleo with our energy and our desires, we each did our individual readings. Ironically enough the readings turned out to be essentially the same for all of us. In order to get the essence of divinatory power that Miss Cleo had we needed to work on aspects of ourselves that would open us up more. This makes sense if you think about it. In order to be a good seer you need to be open-minded and hearted so that you can perceive what others would ignore. We did a bit of numeral divination based off the numbers on our readings and we all received the same number: 7. (Incidentally, in numerology the number seven represents spiritual power, particularly divination.) Finally we burned the images of Miss Cleo and in doing so gave something of ourselves to the Miss Cleo entity in return for what she'd given us.

Now you might realize that working with this kind of entity is a bit different from the other kind we've described. Think of this as an advanced working. We were improving ourselves by working with the entity and we were empowering the entity to make it into a goddess form. By doing so, we were in a different relationship, a different experiment, with an entity, but nonetheless this is an entity working, because most of the impetus for the entity came from first David and myself working together and later Amanda joining us. Bearing all that in mind what we're saying is that each entity is made by you and has it's own value for you. What you choose to do with it can change you, for better or for worse, but it is worth it to create and work with entities as not only a means of doing effective magick, but also as a means of changing yourself and your concepts of reality.

# Appendix H

## The Scents of Magick
*by Amanda R. Wagener*

Much has been published about the healing applications of scent such as aromatherapy, but the magickal applications have been less notable. Much of this is due to the lack of information regarding aroma in ritual. Most consider the other four more physical senses (touch, taste, feeling, sight) to be more important than smell. Magi should not allow themselves to fall into this trap. Scents can be used in our incenses and fragrant oils, not just for ambience, but also to condition us to react on another level. Scent can give subtle suggestions, unlike the other senses.

A reaction of some type happens with all scents on some level. The scents of lavender and chamomile, almost no matter who smells them, tend to cause feelings of relaxation or sleepiness. Rosemary tends to wakes people up. The smell of motor oil may remind you of the racetrack where you used to watch the stock car races with your father. One does not need to think only about "natural" aromas such as the herbs previously mentioned, but also think about the "modern" scents as well, such as gasoline and disinfectant spray. I had a sip of a lemon flavored alcoholic beverege, and the flavor reminded me of the scent of a lemon scented cleaning product, which made me not want to drink it.

Each day in our everyday lives, we are affected by the stimuli of the scents we come across. The most obvious and sensually stirring scents are those that are unusual or unfamiliar. If you are more of an urban dweller, traveling out to a more rural area may fill our nose with many unfamiliar scents. We may be taken by the smell of the newly cut hay or assaulted by the piercing odor of a pig barn. In a strange environment, every smell seems to linger a bit longer and be so much stronger. We are fascinated by every scent, both foul and pleasant.

Now, incorporate these scents into your magick working. If you wish your lover to "get in the mood" when he gets into bed, you can let the scents subtly work their magick into your lover's unconscious. A few drops of patchouli or sandalwood oil may be added to the laundry. While it is diluted enough by the wash water to avoid oil stains and overpowering aromatic evidence, the subtle residue continues to influence your lover. Or, you could also dilute oil or use floral water in a spray bottle and lightly mist bed sheets. Scents such as Cinnamon, Clary sage, Ginger, Jasmine, Neroli, Nutmeg, Patchouli, and Sandalwood to name a few are known for their aphrodisiac properties. Or, try adding a little cinnamon when you brew that next pot of coffee.

Experiment with the various methods of using scent. You can burn herbs or incense or use essential oils or floral waters. You can use scents in massage oils, perfumes, spray bottles, anointing oils, baths, or shampoo. Become acquainted with the nature of each scent in each of its forms. Some scents smell different when you burn them rather than use them as an essential oil. It is best to start with a few herbs before adding more to your repertoire. To start 2–4 herbs are best.

If you wish to burn herbs, make sure you understand the herb. Some are poisonous when burned. Burn each herb separately to become acquainted with the individual nature of each.

If you are going to use essential oils directly on the skin, be aware that some may irritate the skin. You may wish to mix the essential oils with a carrier oil such as almond, coconut, corn, jojoba, olive, sunflower, or safflower.

Scents can be used in tandem with candle magick by anointing the candle with a scent congruent with the purpose of your magickal working. You can use scented water to wash your clothes to uplift your spirits or draw certain people close to you. You can add scents to the water you use to clean your house. Scents be used to activate a sigil or a magickal entity. There are multitudes of ways you can incorporate scents into your magickal workings, you only need to be creative and discover the uses of scents.

With my Inspiration Entity (Emer Ipsni), I used the scent of lemon to call it. The smell of lemon is fresh and tends to wake up the mind. The scent makes me want to do things. Additionally, lemons are yellow, which was the color associated with the entity. When I smell lemon, I think of yellow, so my correspondences were all in alignment. How I used the scent of lemon with my entity was that whenever I opened the bottle that held the scent and smelled it, that activated my entity. Due to my scent association, I would feel like I "needed" to do something, my mind was clearer, and I was ready to work on my creative task.

# GLOSSARY

**Astral**: Consisting of a spiritual substance held in mystical teachings to be next above the tangible world in refinement.

**Balancing**: A ritual act in where the surrounding energy is brought into harmony with the magickal practitioner and the purpose of the ritual.

**Closing By Watchtower**: A ritual act that is used to end rituals. It is common for Ceremonial Magi to use this ritual act.

**Divination**: The art or practice that seeks to discover hidden knowledge, usually by the interpretation of omens or with the aid of divinatory tools such as Tarot cards, Runes, tea leaves, dice, etc.

**Energy**: There is no precise Western definition for the occult understanding of energy. Energy, the phenomena coming forth from the universe and the mind in harmony, is the basic unit of the universe. Ultimately everything is composed and originates from energy. It can be accumulated, focused, and transferred from one person or object to another. Electricity and magnetism are characteristics of energy, which flows in and through all living things. When this circulation becomes stagnant or stops, the person or animal will become ill or die.

**Entity**: A vital principle held to give life to an immaterial essence, which has been created to have a self-contained and distinct existence with a conceptual reality, by the deliberate effort of personifying segregated thoughts and emotions.

**Evocation**: The act of bringing an entity from its plane of existence into your realm of awareness.

**Golem**: From Hebrew folklore—An artificial human being that has been magickally endowed with life.

**Invocation**: The act of allowing an entity to use your body as a temporary medium to interact with the physical world.

**Kabbalah**: Is a mystical tradition rooted in Judaism, which serves as the basis to most Ceremonial Magick. There are many alternative spellings, for example Kabbalah, Qabalah, Cabala, Qaballah, Qabala, Kaballa (and so on).

**Mage**: A person that studies and practices magick

**Magi**: The plural form of the word mage.

**Middle Pillar**: A ritual act that helps to move energy up and throughout the spine (symbolic of the central column of the Tree of Life, which is a central symbol of the Kabbalah).

**Norse**: Relating to the Norwegian or Scandinavian group of Germanic people, languages, traditions, or all three.

**Numerology**: The study of the occult significance of numbers. The two most common systems of numerology are the Chaldean and the Pythagorean.

**Occult**: Secret or hidden. It often refers to information that is understood to have magickal relation in some form or fashion. It does not mean evil, negative, bad, etc.

**Opening By Watchtower**: A ritual act that is used to begin rituals. It is common for Ceremonial Magi to use this ritual act.

**Programming Symbol**: A symbol designed to subconsciously imprint your desires onto the astral realm, in order to create an entity that will manifest those desires.

**Pythagorean Numerology**: A system of numerology created by the Greek philosopher Pythagoras.

**Runes**: Norse symbols used in magickal workings, as characters of any of several alphabets used by the Germanic peoples from about the third to the thirteenth centuries C.E., and as a divinatory tool.

**Spirit**: *See entity*

**Thought-Form**: Energy that is formed by various thoughts. Many are unintentionally created all the time, but most don't last very long because relatively little energy or further thought is put into them. But when one is deliberately created by magick it can last for quite a long time and can be programmed to cause desired results.

**Vibrate**: A method of saying words loudly that cause not only you, but the universe to vibrate when said. This has the effect of aligning you and your magick to produce the results that you desire. It is possible to vibrate words without making a sound. Some magi like to start with a silent vibration of the word until they feel they can no longer keep silent. Then they vibrate the word aloud.

# Selected Bibliography

Bokser, Ben Zion. The Maharal: The Mystical Philosophy of Rabbi Judah Loew of Prague. Jason Aronson, 1994.

Buckland, Raymond. Practical Color Magick. Llewellyn Publications, 1993.

Campbell, Joseph, and Bill Moyers. The Power of Myth. Doubleday, 1988.

Cronin, Gaynell B., and John J. Rathschmidt. Rituals for Home and Parish. Paulist P, 1996.

Crowley, Aleister, and Austin O. Spare. Now for Reality. Holmes Group, 1990.

Crowley, Aleister. Book 4. Samuel Weiser, 1987.

———. Book of the Law. Samuel Weiser, 1990.

Frazer, James G. Golden Bough. The Macmillan Co., 1922.

———. Man, God & Immortality. Kessinger Company, 1942.

Goodman, Morris. Modern Numerology. Wilshire Book Co., 1978.

Haskins, Jim. Voodoo & Hoodoo. Scarborough House, 1990.

Hine, Phil. Condensed Chaos. New Falcon Publications, 1995.

Jung, Carl G. Jung on Synchronicity and the Paranormal. Routledge, 1997.

———. Process of Individuation: Alchemy. Vol. 1. Banton, 1991.

———. Process of Individuation: Alchemy. Vol. 2. Banton, 1991.

———. Psychology and the Occult. Routledge, 1982.

———. The Archetypes and the Collective Unconscious. Routledge, 1991.

King, Serge. Kahuna Healing. Quest Books, 1983.

Konstantinos. Summoning Spirits. Llewellyn Publications, 1995.

Kraig, Donald M. Modern Magick. Llewellyn Publications, 1992.

———. Modern Sex Magick. Llewellyn Publications, 1998.

LaVey, Anton S. The Satanic Witch. Feral House, 1989.

Mace, Stephen. Addressing Power: Sixteen Essays on Magick and the Politics it Implies. Self-Published, 1996.

———. Nemesis and Other Essays. Self-Published, 2001.

———. Stealing the Fire from Heaven: A Technique for Creating Individual Systems of Sorcery. Self-Published, 1989.

Pajeon, Kala, and Ketz Pajeon. The Candle Magick Workbook. Citadel P, 1991.

Penczak, Christopher. City Magick. Weiser Books, 2001.

Pennick, Nigel. Magical Alphabets. Weiser Books, 1992.

Spare, Austin O. From the Inferno to Zos II. Holmes Group, 1995.

Stein, Guy. Geist oder naturlicher Gedanke. Self-Published, 1982.

Strayhorn, Lloyd. Numbers and You. Ballantine Books, 1990.

The Holographic Paradigm and Other Paradoxes. Ed. Ken Wilber. Shambhala Publications, 1982.

Watson, Nancy B. Practical Solitary Magic. Weiser Books, 1996.

Wayne, M. Thought Forms. Abaxion, 1997.

Wilson, Robert A. Prometheus Rising. New Falcon Publications, 1993.

————. Quantum Psychology. New Falcon Publications, 1993.

Winkler, Gershon. The Golem of Prague: A New Adaptation of the Documented Stories of the Golem of Prague. Judaica P, 1980.

# INDEX

# IDEAS AND SUGGESTIONS WANTED

Do you have an idea for creating magickal entities (maybe one better than anything here) that you'd like to share with the readers in future versions of this book?

If you have a better way of creating and working with entities, please let us know what it is!

Please send it to:

Creating Magickal Entities Ideas
C/O Egregore Publishing
PO Box 572
Perrysburg, OH 43552-0572

or e-mail it to:

Entity-Ideas@EgregorePublishing.com

If we find your thoughts especially helpful and use them in future editions of this book, we'll be pleased to send to you a free autographed copy of "Creating Magickal Entities Workbook," a helpful booklet with checklists and extra worksheets to aid you in magickal entity creation, in return.

# Simply ⊛ Magickal™

Serving the Pagan and Heathen communities. A great source for Occult and Magickal supplies.

Featuring articles, full online colour catalogue of products including ritual tools, aromatherapy, bath and body, statues, and more—all with secure ordering!

- candles
- oil diffusers
- faeries
- bath salts
- swords

- goblets
- dragons
- athames
- incense
- fountains

- daggers
- jewelry
- gargoyles
- chalices
- and more!

Quality products for the mind, body, and spirit for your home, office, or garden.

**www.SimplyMagickal.com**

Info@SimplyMagickal.com

Pagan Owned and Operated

Give a copy of Creating Magickal Entities
to your friends and family

[__]   Yes, I want _____ copies for $16.95 each.

[__]   Yes, I am interested in having David Michael
Cunningham, Taylor Ellwood, Amanda R. Wagener,
or all three, speak or give a seminar to my group or
organization. Please send me information.

Include $4.95 for shipping for one book, and $1.95 for each
additional book. Ohio residents must include $1.06 per
book ordered for sales tax. Canadian orders must include
payment in US funds, with 7% GST added. Payment must
accompany orders. Allow 4 to 6 weeks for delivery.

My check or money order for $_____is enclosed.
Please charge my [__] Visa   [__] MasterCard

Name
_____

Organization
_____

Address
_____

City, State, Zip
_____

Phone                         Email
_____

Card #
_____

Exp. Date                     Signature
_____

Make your check payable and return to
Egregore Publishing
PO Box 572
Perrysburg, OH 43552-0572

www.EgregorePublishing.com
Toll Free (888) 771- 5453
Fax: (253) 498 – 3110

Printed in the United Kingdom
by Lightning Source UK Ltd.
125694UK00001B/94/A